# ISLAM

## VS.

## THE UNITED STATES

NICHOLAS F. PAPANICOLAOU

*Islam vs. the United States*
by Nicholas F. Papanicolaou
Copyright © 2010

Oak Leaves Publishing
375 Star Light Drive, Fort Mill, SC 29715
www.oakleavespublishing.com
1-803-547-8217
1-800-542-0278

International Standard Book Number—978-1-60708-384-9; 1-60708-384-1
Cover Design: Kevin Lepp

Website: www.nicholaspapanicolaou.com
Contact: info@nicholaspapanicolaou.com

 facebook.com/nfpapanic

 twitter.com/nfpapanic

 youtube.com/nfpapanic

# TABLE OF CONTENTS

Author Biography . . . . . . . . . . . . . . . . . . . . . . 5

Acknowledgments . . . . . . . . . . . . . . . . . . . . 6

Introduction . . . . . . . . . . . . . . . . . . . . . . . 7

Chapter One
The Historical Struggle Between Christianity and Islam. . . . 11

Chapter Two
An Enemy Within?. . . . . . . . . . . . . . . . . . . . 25

Chapter Three
President Obama and Islam. . . . . . . . . . . . . . . . 33

Chapter Four
The United States Constitution
and the Founding Documents. . . . . . . . . . . . . . . 37

Chapter Five
The Koran and Sharia Law . . . . . . . . . . . . . . . . 39

Chapter Six
Original Intent. . . . . . . . . . . . . . . . . . . . . . 47

Chapter Seven
Islam in America Today. . . . . . . . . . . . . . . . . . 53

Chapter Eight
The Old Testament and the New Testament. . . . . . . . . 59

Chapter Nine
The Origins of Islamo-Fascism in the Modern Era. . . . . . 63

Chapter Ten
Can The Two Religions Be Reconciled? . . . . . . . . . . . . .71

Chapter Eleven
What Can Be Done?. . . . . . . . . . . . . . . . . . . . . .75

Chapter Twelve
Conclusion. . . . . . . . . . . . . . . . . . . . . . . . . .85

Epilogue . . . . . . . . . . . . . . . . . . . . . . . . . . .89


Appendix One. . . . . . . . . . . . . . . . . . . . . . . . .93

Appendix Two. . . . . . . . . . . . . . . . . . . . . . . . .99

Appendix Three. . . . . . . . . . . . . . . . . . . . . . . 103

Appendix Four. . . . . . . . . . . . . . . . . . . . . . . . 123

Appendix Five . . . . . . . . . . . . . . . . . . . . . . . 125

Appendix Six . . . . . . . . . . . . . . . . . . . . . . . . 131

# AUTHOR BIOGRAPHY

**NICHOLAS PAPANICOLAOU** was born in Athens, Greece. He holds a Bachelor's degree in Economics from Harvard University and a Master's degree from Columbia University School of Business. He has enjoyed an active business career as a ship owner and former controlling shareholder and chairman of Aston Martin Lagonda Holdings Ltd., U.K.

In 2002, he co-founded with Vladimir Yakunin of Russia and J.C. Kapur of India the World Public Forum "Dialogue of Civilizations," an NGO registered in Vienna, Austria (www.wpfdc.com). The WPF brings together seven hundred delegates from more than sixty different countries for four days every year on the island of Rhodes in Greece to openly discuss religious and cultural differences. WPF delegates have included the former prime ministers of India, Algeria, the Czech Republic, Austria, the former Presidents of Lithuania, Bangladesh, Khatami of Iran, Slovakia, Armenia, Yemen, President Mahmoud Abbas of the Palestine Authority, and many other dignitaries, archbishops of the Orthodox Church, Cardinals, Ayatollah Ali Tashkiri of Iran, Chief Rabbis and Chief Muftis.

Mr. Papanicolaou is the worldwide leader of the Knights of Saint John of Jerusalem—The Ecumenical Order. This organization is an Order of Knighthood which is engaged in worldwide charity. Over the last three years, this Order has contributed more than $60 million in medicines and supplies to needy countries, including countries with large Muslim populations such as Pakistan, Indonesia, Liberia, and the Philippines. The Order speaks out when Christians are discriminated against because of their religion.

He has been honored with the grand cross of St. Andrew the First Called of Russia for his work on the dialogue of civilizations, the grand cross of Saint John of Jerusalem, the grand cross of the Imperial Spanish Order of Carlos V, and the gold star of the National Rescue Service of the Ukraine, for his humanitarian work.

# ACKNOWLEDGMENTS

Without my wife Victoria's consent and cooperation, this book would not have been possible.

Her courage in allowing me to tackle a controversial subject, and her faith that God makes all things good have been constant and defining.

Equally defining has been the encouragement and support of Rick Joyner and Lt. General Jerry Boykin. They are both men of strong faith and dedication, first to God and then to our country. They are patriots and believers in people and in the free choices God gave us to make, for better or for worse.

Bill NeSmith and my Editor Debbie Joyner have provided valuable assistance, guidance, and support: Debbie with her expertise in editing books, properly ascribing sources and resolving publishing problems; Bill in helping me find the sources of many of our exhibits and in formatting them. I sincerely thank them both.

A warm and sincere thank-you goes to Mike Jacobs for helping steer me toward historical analogies of what Islam is, especially the similarities to the Shinto religion and way of life.

To Kamal Saleem and other friends, I also say that you have set an example to follow with your courage and determination.

We are brothers, not in hating others, but in praying and hoping for the day when their eyes will be opened and they will feel the Lord's love.

# INTRODUCTION

Islam today comprises some 1.5 billion followers. Of these, and depending on whose figures you believe, some 15 to 20 percent are Arabs. The rest are spread out all over the world, with the largest concentration living in Asia. There are some 630 million Muslims in Indonesia, India, Pakistan, and Bangladesh.

Not all followers of Islam think or act the same way. Some are peace-loving and docile, while others are firebrands who seek not only the death of "infidels," or those who do not espouse Islam, but also their own deaths. They have been schooled in believing that dying for Islam will gain them instant entry into Jinnah, Islam's paradise, along with seventy of their chosen relatives.

Professor Durre Samin Ahmed, of the Center for the Study of Gender and Culture at Lahore University in Pakistan, has labeled Islam's present phase as a Saudi-led "theo-cultural bull-dozer." She distinguishes between "Saudi-sponsored Islam," which is replete with "textural semantics," i.e., a very strict interpretation of the Koran based on Wahhabi theology, and the rest of the Islamic populations of the globe. She also points out that Wahhabism is a form of Islam that has only existed for some two hundred years, while the origins of Islam go back some fourteen hundred years. She has called for the return of Islam to multilateralism based on much more internal dialogue within Islam.

Professor Ahmed's opinion lays bare the fact that the Saudi regime, with all the power that its money gives it, should not be allowed to hijack Islam. Evidently, the Saudi version of Islam, and the inroads it has been able to make into countries in Western Europe and the United States, creates a very dangerous situation. It risks not only destroying relations between Christianity and Islam (not to mention Hinduism, Buddhism, and Judaism vs. Islam), which have been able to peacefully coexist for more than two hundred years but, more ominously, it risks destroying Islam as certain countries in the West give up hope of being able to peacefully coexist with Islam into the future.

Aiding and abetting this sad state of affairs is the work of the Muslim Brotherhood. Founded in 1928 in Egypt, the Muslim Brotherhood seeks to impose by force and terror its version of pan-Islamism. Precise figures on the membership of the Muslim Brotherhood are not available, but it is possible its worldwide numbers exceed 200,000.

It is most unfortunate that in the United States, as well as in Western Europe, Saudi Wahhabism and the activities of the Muslim Brotherhood have taken the leading role in defining Islam. Daily acts of terrorism and the unrelenting undermining of Western democratic and liberal institutions make the rest of us feel threatened and place us on a defensive, belligerent footing.

According to *The Religion of Peace* (www.thereligionofpeace.com), since September 11, 2001, militant Islam has been responsible for no less than 83,500 deaths worldwide. That is a completely unacceptable record of violence, especially in the twenty-first century. The world of the twenty-first century seeks and aspires to leave barbarism behind and not have it burst daily into our lives thanks to the efforts of the destroyers of civilization and multi-culturalism.

This book is not intended to be an attack on Islam. It is intended to expose facts; hard facts that few have been willing to come to terms with to date. We must, or the situation will only continue to deteriorate, and the price for extricating the world from it will go up. It is clear that on their theology, Christianity, Judaism, and the other major religions of the world are not reconcilable with militant Islam, yet on a secular level these religions have been able to peacefully coexist.

# INTRODUCTION

The universal aspirations of humanity, the common values we all share, have been able to create the foundations for our coexistence and for our relative peace. Parents the world over still want to father children from their union, children that will enjoy safety, a good measure of happiness and health, and a good education. It matters little if those parents are Muslim, Christian, Hindu, Jewish, adherents of other religions, or no religion at all. This is our common humanity.

This book is my effort to expose what is wrong and what is being done that will not work to bring a solution to this increasingly dangerous situation, to hold it up for scrutiny, and by so doing, to raise the level of awareness both among Muslims and the adherents of other major religions. Awareness can then act as a control to the message of hate put out both overtly and covertly by the adherents of Saudi Wahhabism and of the Muslim Brotherhood. Where I refer to Muslims in America, I seek to draw a distinction between what I would call militant Islam (of the Wahhabi and Muslim Brotherhood variety), and the more peaceful Muslims who far outnumber them.

The faith of 1.5 billion people cannot be discounted, but neither should the acts and money of some 26 million adherents of Islam in Saudi Arabia be allowed to poison mankind. To stop that poison from spreading, non-Muslims need to awaken to the danger, and Muslims need to open effective and result-oriented dialogue between themselves. They must also better control who speaks on their behalf. Such control can take many forms, from speaking openly and with conviction against the forces of regression within their ranks, to actually separating themselves, by force if necessary, from such efforts.

We are all God's creation. We were not intended to be fighting and killing each other, though we seem to have an incredible capacity for doing this; it all began when there were just two brothers on the whole earth. Though I have sought to be strict in setting forth the facts, it is with the hope that truth will set us free and lead to solutions. May God bless and forgive us all.

*Nicholas F. Papanicolaou*

# CHAPTER ONE

# THE HISTORICAL STRUGGLE BETWEEN CHRISTIANITY AND ISLAM

We ignore history at our own peril. If we want to have guidance about future courses of action, we must always look to the past to understand how certain cultures and religions have behaved and are likely to behave in the future.

## ISLAM IN THE EARLY MIDDLE AGES

Islam first appeared on the map in 610 A.D. Muhammad, the prophet and father of Islam, had his visions in Mecca thereby creating a new religion. He was chased out of Mecca, took refuge in Medina, where in time he reared an army. In the beginning, his revelations sounded peaceful (Mecca periods), but when he acquired his army, the revelations changed, and his religion became militant.

He then unleashed an unprecedented torrent of fear, bloody conquest, and forceful conversion. In 629 A.D., the Byzantine Emperor Heraclius, who had rediscovered the Holy Cross, was in Jerusalem when he received the following letter: "In the name of Allah, the most Beneficent, the most merciful: this letter is from Muhammad, the slave of Allah, and his Apostle, to Heraclius, the ruler of the Byzantines. Peace be upon the followers of guidance. I invite you to surrender to

Allah. Embrace Islam and Allah will bestow on you a double reward. But if you reject this invitation, you will be misguiding your people." Emperor Heraclius did not know who this upstart prophet was, who was calling on him to abandon the Holy Cross of Jesus. Pretty soon Islam was laying siege to the gates of Europe, attacking the Byzantine Empire on the east and the soft underbelly of Europe in Spain, France, Greece, and Italy. Almost immediately after his death, it also attacked the Persian Empire to the east and Armenia to the northeast. The Byzantine Empire, headquartered in Constantinople, stood alone protecting the eastern flank of Christian Europe from 700 A.D. until 1453 A.D. when it fell to the Ottoman Turks. The Turks were an Islamic empire and simultaneously the center of the Caliphate. The Mediterranean had become an unsafe sea, where Muslim pirates based on the Barbary Coast in North Africa operated at will, taking Christian ships hostage and selling Christians into slavery. By the sixteenth century A.D., the situation in the Mediterranean was so desperate that 20,000 Christians were being abducted by Muslim pirates every year from the coastal zones of Greece, Italy, France, and Spain and sold into slavery in the bazaars of Algeria. Nothing, and no one, was safe. The Christian kingdoms of Europe eventually attempted to band together in the First Crusade in 1095 A.D. to counterattack and limit the expansion of Islam, and to retake Jerusalem.

Let us pause here to properly address another point of grave misinformation: Militant Muslims repeatedly claim that they took up arms to fight the Crusaders. The implication is that the Crusaders were the first aggressors.

Nothing can be further from the truth. Let us look at the facts about the Muslim conquests:

- Egypt was conquered by the forces of Islam in 647 A.D., then Damascus.

- Cyprus first conquered by the armies of Islam in 653 A.D. (liberated in 965 A.D. by the Byzantine Empire).

- Armenia was conquered in 653 A.D.

- Constantinople was first attacked by the forces of Islam in 678 A.D. The attacking army was defeated and withdrew.

- Constantinople again laid siege in 717 A.D. by a Muslim force of 80,000 men and 1,500 ships. The siege was lifted after the Muslim fleet was again destroyed by "Greek Fire," a mixture of liquid petroleum and sulfur invented by the Byzantines.

- Andalusia and Granada, Spain conquered in 711 A.D. (liberated in 1492 by Ferdinand and Isabella).

- Avignon, France conquered in 719 A.D.

- Paris threatened in 732 A.D. King Thierry IV and Charles Martel defeated the Muslim army 150 miles south of Paris.

- Poitiers, France conquered in 733 A.D.

- Sicily conquered in 828 A.D.

- Malta conquered in 870 A.D. (liberated in 1090 A.D. by the Normans).

- Taranto, Bari, and Brindisi in Italy conquered 840-841 A.D.

- Provence in France, conquered in 889 A.D. all the way to French Alps.

Indeed, Muslim aggression and conquests had turned the Mediterranean Sea into a Muslim lake well before the First Crusade, which started in 1095 A.D.

## ISLAM IN THE MIDDLE AGES

By the mid-1450s, the former Byzantine Empire was in the hands of the Ottoman Turks. The eastern flank of Christian Europe lay unprotected. The result was that by 1683 A.D., the Ottomans laid siege to Vienna itself. All the lands from the eastern Mediterranean Sea to Vienna had already fallen to the forces of Islam.

The Ottomans had also made mutual plundering pacts with the Muslim pirates of North Africa. A pirate called Barbarossa was based in Tripoli, Libya and operated in the mid-sixteenth century under the protection of the Ottoman Sultans.

Cyprus, Rhodes, and Sicily had all fallen to Islam. Only Malta, reconquered from Islam by the Christian Normans in 1090, stood free under the courageous leadership of the Knights of Saint John of Jerusalem, also known as the Knights of Malta.

Finally the Holy Roman Emperor, Charles V, decided that he must put a stop to all of this. He reigned over Spain, Belgium, Luxembourg, the Netherlands, the Kingdom of Naples, and the Two Sicilies, Germany, and Austria from 1516 to 1555. He used the gold that he was mining in the New World to build fleets and armies to oppose Islam. By 1571, his son, Philip II of Spain (1555-1598), had built up a fleet of some two hundred galleys. Charles V also had fielded Christian armies on continental Europe to oppose the allies of the Ottomans.

The allies of the Ottomans were the kingdoms of France and England. King Charles IX of France (1560-1574) even gave free use of France's main naval base at Toulon to the Ottomans and converted the Cathedral of Toulon into a mosque to accommodate the Muslim fleets!

Another indirect but de facto ally of the Ottomans was Queen Elizabeth I of England (1533-1603). It was her pirate flotillas, captained by Sir Francis Drake, that plundered the Spanish galleys coming back to Spain from the New World loaded with gold. The gold stolen from Spain was gold no longer available to build navies with which to fight Islam. Even so, Charles V, and his son Philip II, persevered.

On October 7, 1571 the naval Battle of Lepanto, one of the ten most important naval battles ever, took place off the coast of Patras in western Greece.

Three days before the battle, the Christian crews and commanders were solidified in their resolve through news that came from Cyprus. The Venetian stronghold of Famagusta had fallen on August 17 to the forces of the Ottoman Sultan. His commander, Lala Mustapha, had had the Venetian commander of Famagusta, General Bragadin, tortured in the most hideous way after he had surrendered. After repeatedly tempting him to convert to Islam in order to be saved, offers which Bragadin had refused saying that he was a Christian, Bragadin was beaten and then skinned alive while tied to a column at the entrance of his city. His skin had then been stuffed and his effigy had been paraded around the conquered city. Even while being tortured by the Turks, Bragadin kept praying aloud to God to save the souls of the conquerors.

At Lepanto, under the command of Don Juan of Austria, who was a son of Emperor Charles V, some two hundred Christian galleys met and opposed more than three hundred Ottoman and Muslim galleys. On that day, in four hours of battle, forty thousand men lost their lives. One hundred ships were destroyed, another one hundred and thirty-seven Muslim ships were captured, and nearly twelve thousand Christian slaves, who were forcibly serving on the Muslim ships, were liberated. The battle was witnessed by the young Spanish author, Miguel de Cervantes, who was wounded in the battle and maimed in his left hand. He subsequently wrote that the battle was "the greatest event witnessed by ages past, present, and to come."

As the two fleets were about to join battle with one hundred-fifty frontline armed galleys plowing into each other, the Christian fleet hoisted flags of Jesus and sang hymns. Don Juan was seen kneeling in prayer in his shiny armor on the deck of his flagship, *The Real*. The battle was so fierce that the sea was reported to have been red with blood for days.

At a critical point in the battle, when the Genovese Admiral Andrea Doria made a serious tactical error, six Knights of Malta galleys turned the tide in favor of the Christian navies. The dream of Charles V finally came to pass, and the cleaning up of the Mediterranean began.

The omens had been clear on that day too. It is said that Sultan Selim's turban fell off twice while he was on his way from Constantinople to Eridne, and that his horse had stumbled and fallen from under him. At the battle site, observers are said to have seen black crows fall out of the sky and onto the Muslim fleet outside of Patras, Greece.

## THE RISE OF WAHHABISM AND THE SAUDIS

Wahhabism is a strict reform movement within Islam, which began in the early eighteenth century and was led by Muhammad ibn Abd al-Wahhab. Wahhab rejected the worship of holy men within Islam, advocated strict punishment under what has come to be known as Sharia law and, most importantly, denounced those who believed that Allah could be part of any polytheistic worship. The "oneness of God" was paramount in his teachings. In other words, he believed that Allah's personality was uniquely monotheistic, and therefore denounced those within Islam who worshipped saints or holy men, alongside Allah.

It follows that to Wahhabis, the concept of the Holy Trinity, which Christians worship, is obnoxious and heretical. They are strict believers in Sura 5:73, which denounces the Trinity.

In 1744-45, al-Wahhab made a strategic alliance with Muhammad ibn Saud, the leader of a military clan who was fighting an opposing tribe, the Rashidis, for control of Riyadh. This agreement, known as the Dir'iyya Agreement, bound the followers of al-Wahhab to what came to be the Saudi royal clan. In return for the support of the Wahhabis, the Saudi clan pledged themselves to be their followers and to do all in their power to further this particular brand of creed within Islam and to the rest of the world.

The Wahhabis presented an immediate challenge with their jihadi zeal to the Ottoman Empire which ruled the Arabian peninsula in the eighteenth and nineteenth centuries. So much so, that from 1811 to 1818 a very bloody campaign was waged by the Ottomans' proxy, Ibrahim Pasha of Egypt, to defeat the Wahhabis. Ibrahim succeeded in 1818, and the Wahhabi leaders were publicly beheaded in Istanbul under Sultan Selim I.

However, Wahhabism was to rear its head again in the twentieth century. A descendant of Muhammad ibn Saud, Abd al-Aziz ibn Abd al-Rahman al-Feysal Al Saud, began a storm of conquests in 1902, under the worried gaze of both the Ottoman and the British Empires. In 1902, he and a group of nineteen followers stormed the mud walls of Riyadh at night and wrested the town yet again from the Rashid clan. Ibn Saud had taken the precaution to renew his ancestor's pledge to the Wahhabi leaders, so he managed to hang on to Riyadh and, in fact, began to build a small army with which to pursue further conquests. It must be noted that the nineteen "ikwan," or brothers, that joined him in taking Riyadh in 1902, were almost all cousins or nephews of his. In 1913, ibn Saud conquered further territory, the Hasa region from the Ottomans. Then in June 1918, ibn Saud took the oasis town of Khurma which had hitherto belonged to Sharif Husayn, the Hashemite king of the Hejaz within which lie both Mecca and Medina. He used guns and funds that he had gained from the British to do this, though these guns and funds had been given to him under a treaty signed in 1915 by the British to fight the Ottomans who had entered World War I as Britain's enemies. The conquest of Khurma opened hostilities between the two Arabian kings, ibn Saud and Sharif Husayn. Every town or territory conquered by Saud and his Wahhabi followers was treated cruelly if its inhabitants did not acknowledge Wahhabism. So Arab Muslims were killing, pillaging, and mistreating fellow Arab Muslims, all in the name and for the glory of Wahhabism. As we shall see, it is this same form of fanatical Wahhabism that propels the Saudis, heavily buoyed with the West's petrodollars.

Ibn Saud's campaigns finally led to the conquest of Mecca itself from the Hashemites in October 1924. The British Empire remained passive in the face of this aggression, and the result was that the House of Saud now came to control Islam's holiest place. The conquest of Jiddah and Medina, Islam's second holiest city, followed in January 1925. With that the House of Saud became the most prominent kingdom in Arabia, while the Hashemite royal family who had actually helped the British during World War I, were resettled to Jordan as kings of that territory.

## THE UNITED STATES IS FORCED TO ENTER THE FRAY AGAINST ISLAM

Contrary to the implicit message of President Obama in Cairo that somehow Islam has had a benevolent part "in America's story," it is fair to say that Islam was the first enemy of the new American republic. Islamic piracy, motivated by both greed and religion as we shall see below, led to the victimization of U.S. citizens and commerce, and the first use of force by the U.S. on foreign soil.

It is often said with pride that Morocco was the first nation to recognize the independence of the United States. What were Morocco's motives? Was there an affinity of people, of religion, of culture with the United States? No. The main motive was that by recognizing the United States as an independent nation, U.S. commerce and ships were now open prey for Moroccan pirates who were no longer bound by their treaties with the British Empire. Those treaties had protected American ships while America was still a colony of the British Empire. But now America was on its own, and Morocco made certain that this would be so by quickly recognizing the new nation's independence. It was now open season on American ships, citizens, and property.

The cleaning up of Muslim piracy in the Mediterranean was finally accomplished in 1805. By whom? By the newly-founded Christian republic, the United States of America. Presidents prior to Thomas Jefferson had been paying annual tribute to the Barbary pirates to guarantee safe passage to American ships and lives in the Mediterranean.

After 1776, the newborn republic, not yet having a strong navy to project into the Mediterranean, resorted to paying the Barbary pirates an annual tribute. It made peace treaties with the Islamic pirate regimes in March 1796 with Algeria, in June 1796 with Tunis, and in November 1797 with Tripoli.

By 1795, the U.S. government was paying more than one million dollars in annual tribute to the Barbary pirates. Imagine what the equivalent of that sum would be in today's dollars!

The tributes and the peace treaties did not work.

The attitude of Islam then, as now, was to wage unremitting war on Christians. I will quote, as an example, the joint report by two U.S. Ambassadors to the Continental Congress. Both of these ambassadors went on to become Presidents of the United States. In 1786, Thomas Jefferson (then U.S. Ambassador to France) and John Adams (then U.S. Ambassador to Great Britain) met in London with Sidi Haji Abdul Rahman Adja, then Ambassador of Tripoli to Great Britain. The subject of the meeting was the continuing piracy of the Muslim pirates against American ships and lives in the Mediterranean. In their report to Congress, Ambassadors Jefferson and Adams relayed the response of Tripoli's ambassador to their pleas for peace and safe commerce.

Speaking for the Tripoli "government," Ambassador Adja said:

> "That it was founded on the Laws of their Prophet, that it was written in their Qur'an, that all nations who should not have acknowledged their authority were sinners, that it was their right and duty to make war upon them (i.e., the infidels) wherever they could be found, to make slaves of all they could take as prisoners, and that every Musselman (Muslim) who should be slain in battle was sure to go to paradise."

In 1793 alone, Algerian pirates took ten American merchant-men captive, selling the passengers and crew into slavery. And then there were still Tunisian, Moroccan, and Tripolitan pirates to worry about. Commodore John Paul Jones, the naval hero of the U.S. War of Independence, was even appointed Special Envoy to Algiers in the vain hope that he could help stanch the pirates' depredations on Americans, but nothing worked. In addition, the newly founded republic had also made a terrible miscalculation: Congress had eliminated the fighting Navy in 1785 once the War of Independence was over. Now there was no protection for Americans on the high seas. Recognizing its mistake, in March 1794, the U.S. Congress finally authorized the building of six new frigates, and thus reestablished the U.S. Navy. The frigates subsequently built were the *USS United States, USS Constellation, USS Constitution, USS Congress, USS Chesapeake,* and the *USS President.*

To further correct its previous strategic mistake, in the period between 1794 and 1801, the United States built a total of forty-five new ships for its Navy. It also captured eighty-five ships from the French, with whom the U.S. had been in a quasi war, between 1797 and September 1800. The United States now had the necessary power, but was still reluctant to use it against the pirates. It still needed to learn that appeasement with the forces of piracy, inspired and justified by Islam, does not work. Can we believe that much has really changed since then in the militant Muslim mind?

America continued to pay an annual tribute to the Barbary pirates, hoping to accommodate rather than exacerbate the situation. For example, in September 1800, the frigate *USS George Washington,* commanded by Captain William Bainbridge, delivered into Algiers the annual tribute. The contempt of the Dey of Algiers for America was such that he ordered the *USS George Washington* to fly the Algerian flag and to deliver for him presents destined for the Sultan of the Ottomans in Constantinople. Captain Bainbridge was forced to comply with these demands, lest the Americans being held hostage by the Dey be harmed. Captain Bainbridge managed, somehow, to retain what dignity he could through this ordeal. In October 1800, he sailed into Constantinople flying the Algerian flag as ordered by the Dey. Apparently he did make a positive impression on the Turks, who took note of America and its fighting men for the first time. In May 1801, Tripoli had opened "official" hostilities against the United States, because the tribute from the U.S. was paid late! The *USS President, USS Philadelphia, USS Essex,* and *USS Enterprise* were immediately dispatched to the Mediterranean to protect American property and lives.

In 1804, President Thomas Jefferson would finally have no more of it. He ordered the U.S. Navy and Marines into Tripoli. In a series of engagements, lasting from February 16, 1804 to May 27, 1805, the U.S. Navy and Marine Corps conquered Tripoli and put an end to piracy. Lt. Stephen Decatur, Lt. C. Stewart, Lt. Isaac Hull, Lt. J. Smith, Master Commodore Isaac Chauncey, Commodore Edward Preble, and other valiant officers captained seventeen U.S. Navy ships used in this operation. Many of the glorious names of the ships used in the operations of 1804-1805 are still in use today, including the *USS Constitution, USS Intrepid, USS Nautilus, USS Argus, USS John Adams, USS Enterprise, USS Hornet,* and *USS Constellation.* Opposing the U.S. fleet was a pirate force of twenty-five ships and twenty-five thousand men. Fighting was heavy.

In February 1804, Lt. Stephen Decatur had the courage to enter Tripoli harbor on the *USS Intrepid* and burn the *USS Philadelphia,* which had earlier been captured by the pirates when she ran aground. The great admiral, Lord Horatio Nelson, labeled Lt. Decatur's feat "the most bold and daring act of the age." A fundamental tenet of naval warfare is that a naval ship must not expose itself to shore-based fire. Yet Lt. Decatur did just that and managed to accomplish his mission.

In May 1805, the U.S. even landed Marine detachments in Alexandria under the command of Lt. Presley O'Bannon, who marched west across five hundred miles of desert and attacked Tripoli from the rear, while the Navy and the Marines made frontal attacks from the sea.

On May 27, 1805, the U.S. flag was raised over the fortress of Derna, outside Tripoli, and piracy was finished. This engagement marked the first time that the U.S. flag was raised on foreign soil and also the first time that U.S. power was projected abroad. This is why the United States Marine Anthem begins with "From the halls of Montezuma to the shores of Tripoli."

What is my point in taking us through this review of history?

Much Christian blood was spilled to secure our freedoms: our freedom from being forcibly converted to Islam; our freedom from both physical and spiritual slavery. Today, we are unthinkingly relinquishing those freedoms back to militant Islam, in the name of political correctness, and under the leadership of mindless politicians whose agendas may not yet be fully understood.

## ISLAM IN JERUSALEM

Jerusalem is a special case. As the spiritual and historical center of Judaism and Christianity, its conquest by Islam in 638 A.D. is of particular significance. Christians are repeatedly told in Scripture that Jerusalem is God's city. Jews are told the same. Yet we often hear the claim that Jerusalem is also a holy city of Islam. Does Islam have any legitimate religious origins in Jerusalem? What are the historical facts?

During the life of Christ, Jerusalem was the capital of a Roman province. In 70 A.D., the Romans sacked it, destroyed the Second Temple, and ended Jerusalem's quasi-autonomy under the Roman Empire. In 313 A.D., the Roman Emperor Constantine the Great (306-336 A.D.) moved the capital of the empire from Rome to the city of Byzantium, which he renamed Constantinople. At the same time, he declared Christianity the official religion of the Empire. Jerusalem thus was part of the Christian Byzantine Empire. In the year 326 A.D., Constantine's mother, the Empress Helena, who was Greek and had led her son to Christianity, visited Jerusalem. She had excavations done and discovered the Holy Cross. In 335 A.D., the Church of the Holy Sepulcher was completed by Constantine. Jerusalem remained in Christian hands until 638 A.D. when the second Caliph, Umar ibn al-Khattab, conquered it.

Let us remember that the prophet Muhammad had died in 632 A.D., and six years later the wave of violence and conquest that Islam had unleashed had led to the conquest of Jerusalem. When Caliph Umar entered the Holy City, he visited the Church of the Holy Sepulcher, but refrained from praying inside. According to Islamic tradition, if he had prayed inside the church, it would have become a mosque. Instead, he visited the site where the Second Temple, built by King Herod the Great (35 B.C. to 4 A.D.), had stood. It had been left as a heap of rubble—broken stones from the Roman destruction in 70 A.D. He decided to build the mosque known as the Dome of the Rock on the Temple Mount, exactly over the site of the Temple of Solomon and the Second Temple. The Al-Aqsa Mosque followed some three hundred years later on a site close by.

How can Islam lay any sort of legitimate claim to Jerusalem as a holy city of Islam when Muhammad was never there and Islam's origins are in Medina and Mecca?

The only claim of Muhammad's presence in Jerusalem ever made by Islam is that, somehow, the 18th Sura called "The Night Journey", must refer to a night visit by Muhammad to Jerusalem on a winged mule, though the city is never named.

Any claim of Islam to Jerusalem is not based on theology but on bloody conquest. A symbol of conquest typical of Islam is the mosque built over Israel's most holy site, the Temple of Solomon. And, it must be noted, that Jerusalem did not remain under Islam forever. During the period from 1099 to 1187 it was a Christian kingdom, then again from 1229 to 1244 under Frederick II of Germany, and then again from 1917 to 1948 as a protectorate of the British Empire. If one looks at the history of Jerusalem from its very beginning, when it is mentioned as Salem in the Old Testament, it has been under the rule of Islam for only 1,279 years out of its more than four thousand year-old history.

# CHAPTER TWO
# AN ENEMY WITHIN?

In November 2001, a document was seized in the home of a Mr. Youssef Nada in Lugano, Switzerland. The document was written in 1982 and titled, "Toward a Worldwide Strategy for Islamic Policy." It was the Muslim Brotherhood's road map to acquiring, in measured steps, control over the thinking and expansion of Islam into the West. It outlines twelve Points of Departure, with escalating significance.

For example, the First Point of Departure called for the creation of "centers of study and research" to "produce studies on the political dimension of Islamic movement." This has already been accomplished in America with overlapping research centers at major universities such as Harvard.

The Fourth Point of Departure calls for "liberty to function politically." Liberal laws in Western democracies, coupled with a false principle of political correctness, have provided the "liberty" sought by the Muslim Brotherhood (M.B.), with which they intend to deny us ours. The same Fourth Point calls for participation by Muslims in local and national governments. In many European countries, this has already been achieved with Muslims who are members of Parliament and even ministers in the government, including the United Kingdom's previous labor government. In the United States, the first Muslim member of the House of Representatives was elected in 2008. These Muslims may not all be labeled militant Islamists. On the other hand, where are the denunciations of militant Islam and of terror that we are entitled to expect from them? And what is their actual background and previous affiliations?

The Fifth Point calls for Muslims "to work with influential institutions and use them in the service of Islam." As we will see below, Harvard Law School's Islamic Finance Project (IFP), financed by Abu Dhabi Islamic Bank, HSBC Amanah Bank, and Kuwait Finance House, has been instrumental in getting Sharia-Compliant Finance introduced into America. The IFP project is but one of the various Islamic studies centers within Harvard, let alone other centers financed by the Saudis and others which have been established at other U.S. universities. The Fifth Point also calls for the drawing up of "an Islamic Constitution" and of "Islamic laws, civil laws, etc."

The Eighth Point cautions Muslim activists to "not look for confrontation with our adversaries, at the local or global scale" because such confrontations "could encourage its adversaries to give it (i.e., the Islamic movement) a fatal blow."

The Ninth Point calls for the establishment of an autonomous security force to protect the Dawa and its disciples locally and worldwide. So now we are talking about a private Muslim worldwide security force in contravention of the laws of various nations!

The Tenth Point calls for the use of "surveillance systems, in several places, to gather information and adopt a single effective warning system serving the worldwide Islamic movement." It also calls for "creation of an effective and serious media center."

The Eleventh Point of Departure instructs "to adopt the Palestinian cause as part of a worldwide Islamic plan, with the policy plan and by means of jihad, since it acts as the keystone of the renaissance of the Arab world today." It also calls for comparative studies of the Crusades and of Israel, the goal presumably being to equate the two as forces of evil.

It ends by setting as an objective "to nourish a sentiment of rancor with respect to the Jews and refuse all coexistence." It appears that we are now at the Eleventh Point of this strategic plan!

Let us also note the cold calculation of using the Palestinian issue as a springboard for worldwide jihad against Christians and Jews.

## Legitimizing Islamic Finance in the United States

President Bush's Treasury Department held in April 2002 the first "Islamic Finance 101" Seminar, led by Under Secretary for International Affairs John B. Taylor.

The ill thought-out rationale for opening the door to Islamic finance in the U.S. was, as stated in that seminar, that "lawful and legitimate institutions such as conventional banks, Islamic banks, money transfer services, hawalas, and charities must not be abused by terrorists." The seminar was "the result of a collaborative effort between the Treasury Department and the Harvard Islamic Finance Information Program."

Then on June 2, 2004, the Treasury Department adopted its first Islamic Finance Scholar-in-Residence program. The purpose of the program is "to promote broader awareness of Islamic finance practices, internationally and domestically, for U.S. policymakers, regulators, and the public at large."

Dr. Mahmoud El-Gamal, chaired professor of Islamic Economics, Finance and Management and professor of Statistics and Economics at Rice University, was appointed to serve as the first Scholar-in-Residence. So, the initial objective, which was to learn about the practices of Islamic finance so as to close the door on financing terrorism had by now been co-opted to also "promote broader awareness" by not only regulators but also by "the public-at-large." If the intent was to stop terrorists from using the financial system for financing their activities, I can see the need for regulators' awareness to be raised. But the public-at-large? What role could the pubic-at-large be expected to play in the fight against Islamic terrorism by disseminating to it the principles and practices of Sharia-Compliant Finance?

Does this all sound a bit like a Trojan horse policy, whose real intent may be to introduce into the U.S.A., and to legitimize, Sharia-Compliant Finance? Additionally, a simple question comes to mind: Were not the banking and finance rules of the United States adequate and helpful in creating the greatest economy the world has ever known? Is Sharia-Compliant Finance truly a necessary addition to our financial system? Has the U.S. Treasury ever boasted of promoting the understanding of "Christian-Compliant Finance" or of "Torah-Compliant Finance?" Are we witnessing a period of reverse discrimination?

In August 2006, the U.S. Treasury Department's Office of International Affairs published its "Overview of Islamic Finance, Occasional Paper No. 4." The paper was written by Dr. El-Gamal, the U.S. Treasury's Scholar-in-Residence, and provides some astonishing insights. It begins by stating that Islamic finance "started as a small cottage industry in some Arab countries in the late 1970s." While the paper's intended purpose is to review, explain, and "normalize" Islamic finance, the introductory paragraph states: "However, reliable data is not available on Islamic finance at the country, regional or global levels." Well, if reliable data is not available, and Islamic finance started as a cottage industry only in the late 1970s, why is there such pressure to legitimize it in the U.S. as though it were some kind of a major new financial system? Additionally, why is it that Islamic finance only started in the late 1970s, when the Koran and Sharia law have existed since 650 A.D.?

Could the rise in alleged demand for Islamic Finance products be tied somehow to the explosion in crude oil prices (remember the oil shocks of 1973 and 1979) which enriched, empowered, and emboldened Arab oil producers beyond rationality? The paper states on page 8: "Not surprisingly, the rise of Islamic finance in the late 1970s coincided with the two oil shocks of that decade, which created an immense amount of wealth." On the same page, the paper advises us that "the earliest private Islamic banks of the modern era were Dubai Islamic Bank, Faisal Islamic Bank Egypt, and Faisal Islamic Bank Sudan, the latter two being sponsored by Prince Muhammad Al-Faisal, son of the late King Faisal of Saudi Arabia."

The paper begins by explaining the reasons for Muslim opposition to conventional Western banking and insurance products, such as interest-bearing bank accounts, insurance products, interest-earning loans, and mortgages, etc. It mentions that Sharia jurists are opposed to the payment of interest (called riba, or usury in Arabic) and to the purchase of insurance products which is viewed as gambling. It explains, in summary fashion, what alternative products have been developed by banks (including not only Arab-owned banks but Western banks such as Citibank, HSBC, Barclays Bank, UBS, and Credit Suisse).

It then goes on to discuss Islamic scholars' opposition to insurance. In short, opposition arises for two reasons:

a) that "safety" or "insurance" is not in itself viewed as an object of sale in Islamic jurisprudence, and

b) that insurance companies tend to "concentrate their assets in interest-based instruments such as government bonds and mortgage-backed securities," which are unacceptable in Islam because they pay interest.

The paper then advises that Islamic jurists come up with an alternative to the buying and selling of insurance, called "Takaful." Takaful is very similar to mutual insurance "wherein there is no cumulative financial contract that allows one to interpret premium payments as prices and insurance claim fulfillment as an object of sale." "Rather," the paper goes on, "policyholders are viewed as contributors to a pool of money, which they agree voluntarily to share in cases of loss to any of them."

Though I am not an expert on the new Obamacare law, I am reliably informed that Muslims are effectively excluded from mandatory participation and payment into the scheme that will govern all other Americans, while they (Muslim Americans) will be entitled to receive the coverage provided by the Federal Government's health insurance. Page 107 of the Obamacare bill effectively excuses Muslims because Sharia jurists have labeled this type of health insurance as "gambling."

Thus we should wonder: Could the Obama Administration and the U.S. Congress not have tailored the new health bill as a mutual insurance entity, thus obliging Muslim Americans to contribute into it like every other citizen? Was the Obama Administration knowingly doing a favor for American Muslims by tailoring the bill the way it did, thereby giving them a free pass? Is this bill another form of reverse discrimination, where Muslims receive free benefits, while the costs of insuring them must now be paid by the new second-class citizens of America, the Judeo-Christians and other non-Muslims?

The U.S. Treasury's paper, revealingly, goes on to state on page 7: "Consequently, Islamic jurists have invoked the rule of necessity to allow Takaful companies to sell their risks to conventional re-insurance companies, with the provision that they should work to develop a re-Takaful company as soon as possible."

If Islamic jurists can invoke this "rule of necessity" regarding re-insurance, why are they not also invoking it to oblige Muslims to participate in the purchasing of the Obama health care insurance law?

Last, there is a very interesting footnote on page 2 of the paper. It states: "Sharia literally means 'the way' and is the Arabic term for Islamic Law as a way of life...."

As mentioned in Chapter Five, Sharia is a way of life that mandates hard rules, with even harder punishment for disobedience, on all aspects of life. It is fundamentally at odds with the U.S. Constitution and the Declaration of Independence. Here, in the "Overview of Islamic Finance, Occasional Paper No. 4," published by the U.S. Treasury Department in August 2006, we have confirmation by the Treasury's own Scholar-in-Residence that Sharia is "a way of life."

In Matthew 11:15 Jesus says, **"He who has ears to hear, let him hear."**

President Obama has also appointed Arif Alikhan as Assistant Secretary of Homeland Security for Policy Development. Previously, Mr. Alikhan had served as an appointed (not elected) Deputy Mayor of Los Angeles where he used his power to cancel religious mapping of L.A. neighborhoods and other anti-terrorist plans that were being developed by the L.A. Police Department. The announcement of this appointment occasioned, on May 6, 2009, a public announcement from The Council on American-Islamic Relations (CAIR) Director Mr. Hussan Hyloush, congratulating him on his appointment. How is it that Mr. Alikhan keeps getting ever-increasing power, always through appoinment and not through election?

In Chapter 7 we shall see that CAIR has been identified as a front for the Muslim Brotherhood in America. According to John Guandolo, former FBI Special Agent, Counter Terrorism Division, Washington Field Office, CAIR's leadership in 1994 was taken over by Messrs. Omar Ahmad and Nihad Awad, who had until that time served as leaders of IAP (The Islamic Association of Palestine), a well-known Muslim Brotherhood and Hamas front organization in the U.S.

This very same CAIR, which Texas court documents have shown was the fourth Hamas-front entity created in America, was congratulating Mr. Alikhan on his appointment to the Department of Homeland Security. What are we to make of that endorsement?

Incidentally, Special Agent Guandolo was designated by the FBI as a "Subject Matter Expert on the Muslim Brotherhood, the Islamic Movement, and Violent Jihad Organizations."

President Obama has also appointed Mr. Kareem Shora as National Executive Director of the Homeland Security Advisory Council. Born in Damascus, Syria, Mr. Shora has also been described as a devout Muslim, who publicly criticized the CIA for alleged torture of terrorist detainees.

We now also read of Islamic inroads into American education. It has recently been reported that the New York Regents exam on Global History and Geography contained a passage that said wherever Muslims went in the centuries following the birth of Islam, they "brought with them their love of art, beauty, and learning. From about the eighth to the eleventh century, their culture was superior in many ways to that of Western Christendom." Was the "historian" who wrote this referring to the beauty of skinning people alive as we saw previously in this book? Or was he referring to the forced learning that submission to Islam is? When he refers to Islam as "superior in many ways to that of Western Christendom," is he perhaps forgetting the wonders of the Byzantine Empire or the beautiful Christian cathedrals and universities built all over Western Europe?

Our silence enables this type of misinformation.

Late in 2010, the City of Jacksonville, Florida appointed Parvez Ahmed as its Commissioner of Human Rights. Mr. Ahmed was the National Chairman of CAIR from 2005 to 2008. I think it is also legitimate to ask what Mr. Ahmed really believes about human rights and women's rights, given his obvious background with an organization that is an unindicted co-conspirator in the Holy Land Foundation/Hamas case. It is also legitimate to ask what the members of the City Council of Jacksonville are up to with such an appointment.

# CHAPTER THREE
# PRESIDENT OBAMA AND ISLAM

Since the tragic events of 9/11, much attention has been directed to Islam in America. It has not only been the fanatical bombing of the Twin Towers, but a series of subsequent acts such as the American Airlines Shoe Bomber, the Christmas Day Bomber, the Times Square Bomber, Major Nidal Hasan and the Fort Hood massacre, and virtually all other incidents.

Most recently, attention has been centered on the Ground Zero mosque and the imam behind it, Feisal Abdul Rauf. In between these events, we also have been treated to photos of President Obama taking off his shoes to pray at a mosque, but not at a Christian church or a synagogue; Obama declaring in 2007 that America is no longer a Christian nation; Obama declaring on June 4, 2009 in Cairo that "Islam has always been part of America's story;" Obama canceling the National Day of Prayer in May 2010 because of "not wanting to offend anyone;" Obama attending an open-air rally by 50,000 U.S. Muslims outside the White House; Obama's new healthcare bill and the special treatment it accords Muslims on page 107, and then on Friday, August 13, 2010, Obama endorsing the Ground Zero mosque at a special dinner given at the White House for U.S. Muslims. On

*Tribute paid to Barbary pirates.*
*"...the halls of Tripoli"*

top of all this came his iconic book where the President declared that if things got really ugly, he would side with the Muslims.

It is fair to say that President Obama's actions have seriously rattled America.

So, what part of America's story has Islam been? In this book, we shall explore exactly what part of America's story Islam has been.

As a commentator recently observed:

- Did Muslims come to the United States with the pilgrims?
- Did Muslims attend the first Thanksgiving dinner?
- Did Muslims sign the Declaration of Independence?
- Did Muslims sign the United States Constitution?
- Did Muslims sign the Bill of Rights?
- Did Muslims fight in the Civil War to help abolish slavery?
- Did Muslims walk side-by-side with Susan B. Anthony?
- Did Muslims belong to the Women's Suffrage movement that gained the vote for women in this country?
- Did Muslims walk alongside Dr. Martin Luther King during the Civil Rights era?
- Did Muslims lead, as innovators or scientists, in the great medical and scientific inventions of the U.S.A.?

## THE GROUND ZERO MOSQUE

Hand-in-hand with the events enumerated in this book are articles by prominent U.S. Muslims like Feisal Abdul Rauf, the Ground Zero mosque promoter, who stated that "Islamic Law and American democratic principles have many things in common." In an interview on March 27, 2009 with *The Washington Post*, Mr. Rauf stated:

"Thomas Jefferson wrote that the Creator endowed man with these unalienable rights. The framers of the Constitution wrote that they were establishing justice, ensuring domestic tranquility, promoting general welfare, and securing the blessings of liberty. In the same way, Islamic law believes that God has ordained political justice, economic justice, and help for the weak and the impoverished. These are very Islamic concepts . . . American beliefs in individual liberty and the dignity of the individual are Islamic principles as well."

On May 26, 2010, in an interview with Sa'da Abdul Maksoud of the popular Islamic media Hadiyul-Islam, this same Mr. Rauf stated in part:

"Throughout my discussions with contemporary Muslim theologians, an Islamic state can be established in more than just a single form or mold, the important issue is to establish the general fundamentals of Sharia that are required to govern." He went on to say, "new laws are permitted after the death of Muhammad, so long of course that these laws do not contradict the Koran or the Deeds of Muhammad . . . so they create institutions that assure no conflicts with Sharia."

Perhaps Mr. Rauf has not heard that we already have our institutions in the United States such as the U.S. Constitution. We do not need or welcome his new laws to make our country compliant with Sharia law.

During his interview on CNN's *Larry King Live* on September 8, 2010, Mr. Rauf made some additional stunning remarks:

a) He objected to Ground Zero being called "sacred ground," citing as his reason that there are "strip joints" and deli shops in the area. He then went on to say that we need to be "fair" about calling it sacred ground.

b) He repeatedly issued veiled threats that not building the mosque at Ground Zero is now a "national security" issue, that U.S. troops serving abroad and even America itself would now be in greater danger if the mosque is not built at that site. The logical conclusion of his remarks was that America is basically obliged to build the mosque at Ground Zero lest the Muslim world explode in anger.

What about America's exploding in anger over its three thousand dead at Ground Zero?

What about America's right to regulate its own internal affairs without threats from those Muslims for whom Mr. Rauf speaks?

And what about asking ourselves how this man dares to issue such threats and insults, when in the first place he is responsible for getting America into this predicament with his irresponsible proposal for the Ground Zero mosque?

One has to marvel also at the veil of "saintliness" with which Mr. Rauf delivered his comments on CNN. There appears to be very little that was saintly, when his message was one of threats and insults to the sacred ground that is Ground Zero.

We must always be mindful of the fact that Islam is not just a religion; it is a political system, a legal system, a financial system, a banking system, a personal and public hygiene system, and a moral system, all wrapped into a theology. Islam and its child, Sharia (meaning "the Way") are, in fact, a whole-life system.

Seen in the context of Islam as a whole-life system, opposition to the Ground Zero mosque, based on the long arrest record of Mr. Sharif el-Gamal, the owner of the land on which it is to be built, and the $224,270 of unpaid taxes he owes to the City of New York from January 2010, probably pales in significance. Yet it must be noted that Mr. el-Gamal had been arrested as recently as September 10, 2005 for assaulting and injuring a Mr. Vassiliev, to whom he eventually had to pay $15,000 in damages plus late payment fees of $1,360. Previous to that incident, Mr. el-Gamal also apparently had accumulated a record of other problems with the authorities.

It is also noteworthy that Mayor Bloomberg of New York City, in his rush to endorse the mosque, did not even feel the need to stand up for his city and demand that the $224,270 in back taxes owed to it by Mr. el-Gamal's company be paid prior to any consideration being given to the building of this mosque.

How can the Mayor's behavior be understood or condoned?

# CHAPTER FOUR
# THE UNITED STATES CONSTITUTION AND THE FOUNDING DOCUMENTS

L et us look briefly at certain key provisions of these two founding documents of our nation.

## 1) THE DECLARATION OF INDEPENDENCE

*We hold these truths to be self-evident, that all men are created equal, that they are endowed by their Creator with certain unalienable rights, that among these are Life, Liberty, and the Pursuit of Happiness. That to secure these rights, Governments are instituted among Men, deriving their just powers from the consent of the Governed, that whenever any Government becomes destructive of these ends, it is the Right of the People to alter or to abolish it, and to institute new Government....*

We will look more closely at the concept of liberty as understood from the Koran, and also the concept of "governments deriving their just powers from the consent of the governed" as understood and practiced in Islamic countries. We should also consider whether under Islam a government that "becomes destructive of these ends," namely of liberty and the consent of the governed, can in fact be replaced. Can, for example, the government of Iran or of Saudi Arabia be peacefully replaced if it fails to have the consent of the governed? Only a surrealist like Mr. Rauf would dare claim that "American beliefs in individual liberty and the dignity of the individual are Islamic principles as well."

## 2) THE U.S. CONSTITUTION

The introductory paragraph of the Constitution states that to "secure the Blessings of Liberty to ourselves and our Posterity, (we) do ordain and establish this Constitution for the United States of America." Article VI of the Constitution provides that "this Constitution . . . shall be the supreme Law of the Land...."

This leaves no room for Sharia law in America, does it?

## 3) THE AMENDMENTS TO THE U.S. CONSTITUTION

The First Amendment provides that Congress can make no law establishing a religion or prohibiting the free exercise thereof or abridging the freedom of speech. Have you ever heard of freedom of speech, or of religion, in a Sharia-controlled country?

The Fourteenth Amendment provides that no person can be a Senator, Congressman, Elector, Officer in the Armed Forces, or Civil Officer (Federal, State, or Judicial) if they had earlier taken an oath to support the Constitution and subsequently "engaged in insurrection or rebellion against the same."

Does every devout Muslim secretly rebel in his heart, as Major Nidal Hasan evidently did, at the freedoms guaranteed by the U.S. Constitution?

We need to look at how compatible the strict interpretation of the principles of Islam is to the U.S. Constitution. We will also look later in this presentation at how the Founding Fathers, and subsequent Federal and State Supreme Courts, decided such issues.

# CHAPTER FIVE
# THE KORAN AND SHARIA LAW

First let us take a look at what the Koran, certain Hadiths (additional sayings of Muhammad), and Sharia law mandate every devout Muslim should do. This is important to understand because we need to be sure of the truth when apologists for Islam tell us that our religions are very similar and that Islam is a religion of peace. Before we begin, let me emphasize a couple of important principles of Islam:

a) The Prophet Muhammad stated that he received "progressive revelation." He received this revelation during the period from 610 A.D. to 632 A.D., when he died. In the Koran (verse 10:37), Muhammad claims that the archangel, Gabriel, gave him the revelations. The principle of progressive revelation means that the later verses (Surahs) of the Koran, supersede and abrogate the earlier ones. It is therefore important to know which verses were among the last written because, to a devout Muslim, those are the verses that really count. Also, the Koran's verses were not organized into a whole book until 650 A.D. by the then Caliph, Othman. So, it was not Muhammad who put the Koran's verses in their present sequence, but Caliph

Othman. What were the Caliph's motives in presenting the Koran's verses in the particular sequence that he chose?

b) The Koran's verses are not presented in the chronological order in which they were written. Its verses are presented in order of size, i.e., the longest verses are presented first, and the shortest verses come last. Scholars of the Koran know which verses are among the last. In Appendix One, you will find a chronological list of when each Surah of the Koran was written. This research was carried out by Major Stephen Coughlin, United States Army Reserve.

c) Muslims are told that they are blessed when they lie in furtherance of Islam. They have no problem lying to Christians or misleading them when they talk of the true intentions of Islam. This is called the principle of taqiyya, or al-toqiah, in Islam.

The Koran's verses were written in four stages: early Mecca, mid-Mecca, late-Mecca, and Medina. Caliph Othman organized them into 114 verses. You can look these up on Google by typing in "Koran" and the verse number desired.

We will now look more closely at verse 5 (the 112th verse written out of the 114), verse 9 (the 113th written), verse 4 (the 92nd written), and verse 18 (the 69th verse written). In my experience, when a Christian questions a Muslim on the peace supposedly preached by the Koran, he is always pointed to the earlier verses from the Koran. The Muslim knows he is dissimulating, but remember that with taqiyya he is blessed when he lies in furtherance of Islam.

## 1) THE KORAN ON JESUS

From Verse 5:72: "Pagans indeed are those who say that God is the Messiah (note: he means Jesus), son of Mary."

From Verse 5:75: "The Messiah, son of Mary, is no more than a messenger like the messengers before him, and his mother was a saint...."

From Verse 5:73: "Pagans indeed are those who say that God is a third of a trinity."

Note: Contrast this verse from the Koran to Matthew 28:19 where Jesus clearly instructs His apostles to go and baptize the nations **"in the name of the Father, and the Son and of the Holy Spirit."**

From Verse 18:4: "Further that he may warn those who say 'Allah hath begotten a son.'"

From Verse 5:116: "God will say, 'O Jesus, son of Mary, did you say to the people, 'make me and my mother idols beside God?' He will say, 'Be You glorified. I could not utter what was NOT RIGHT...'" (caps are mine). Jesus is *not* God in the Koran, and the Holy Trinity does not exist.

Islamic scholars are so bent on proving that Jesus is not God that they even use John 20:17 in a vain attempt to claim that Jesus Himself admitted He was not God: **"Jesus said to her, 'Stop clinging to Me, for I have not yet ascended to the Father; but go to My brethren and say to them, I ascend to My Father and your Father, and My God and your God.'"** We need to understand, of course, that it was essential for Islam to prove that Jesus is not God because Muhammad's message is so different from Jesus' and Muhammad laid claim only to being a prophet. If Jesus was God, Muhammad has no place as a true prophet. Therefore, Muhammad needed to marginalize Jesus in Islam, to reduce Him to the rank of one of a long line of prophets. Muslims will mention to Christians that the Koran recognizes and honors Jesus, but this assurance is misleading.

Significantly, Muhammad never claimed he was God, and when he did try to skate close to the issue by telling his followers that he would move a mountain, the mountain mysteriously refused to obey.

Muslim scholars misinterpret John 20:17 and simultaneously completely ignore the many passages in the New Testament (see Matthew 16:17; Galatians 4:5), which testify to the deity of Jesus. Yet their apologists, like Mr. Feisal Abdul Rauf, attempt to convince us that our religions are similar and that we worship the same God.

If Jesus is not God in Islam, how can the two religions be said to be worshiping the same God?

## 2) THE KORAN ON RULING THE INFIDELS AND ON DEMOCRATIC INSTITUTIONS

From Verse 5:48: "Then we revealed to you this scripture, truthfully, confirming previous scriptures, AND SUPERCEDING THEM (caps are mine). You shall RULE among them (i.e., the infidels) in accordance with God's revelations, and do not follow their wishes if they differ from the truth that came to you."

From Verse 5:49: "You shall rule among them in accordance with God's revelations to you. Do not follow their wishes, and beware lest they divert you from some of God's revelations to you. If they turn away, then know that God wills to punish them for some of their sins."

## 3) THE KORAN ON PROGRESSIVE REVELATION

From Verse 5:101: "O you who believe, do not ask about matters which, if revealed to you prematurely, would hurt you. If you ask about them in light of the Quran, they will become obvious to you. God has deliberately overlooked them...."

Evidently, the verses above establish that the Koran supersedes all civilian authority, laws, and the U.S. Constitution, if they differ from the Koran. Do you see any potential problems here between being a devout Muslim and abiding by the U.S. Constitution?

Do you also see in these verses the principle that the Koran supersedes all previous Scripture, including the Old Testament and the New Testament?

Do you also see the command that Muslims are to "rule over" us? And finally, do you see that verse 5:101 establishes the principle that the Koran needed to be revealed step-by-step? Evidently, this introduces the concept of progressive revelation, and establishes the principle that newer verses abrogate the older ones.

## 4) THE KORAN ON BUILDING MOSQUES OVER THE INFIDELS

From Verse 18:21: "...Behold, they (i.e., the Muslims) dispute among themselves as to their affair. Some said 'Construct a building over them' (i.e., non-believers, Jews, and Christians): (But) their Lord knows best about them: those who prevailed over their affair said 'Let us surely build a place of worship over them.'"

Muslims are commanded to build mosques over our symbols, our places of worship. Look at the facts: The Temple of Solomon, Hagia Sophia in Constantinople, the Church of the Holy Wisdom of God and Christianity's first cathedral and the Christian cathedrals in Southern Spain (Cordoba, Seville, Segovia, Andalusia, etc.) all were converted to mosques or had mosques built over them. Is there any doubt why Muslims hatched the plan to build a mosque over another one of their perceived "places of victory" at Ground Zero? This is crude triumphalism over all our values, over our Judeo-Christian heritage. Appendix Two provides a list of some prominent Christian churches and Hindu temples which were converted to mosques to mark the triumph of Islam.

## 5) THE KORAN ON JEWS AND CHRISTIANS

From Verse 5:57: "O you who believe, do not befriend those among the recipients of PREVIOUS SCRIPTURE who mock and ridicule your religion, nor shall you befriend the disbelievers."

From Verse 5:51: "O you who believe, do not take certain Jews and Christians as allies; these are allies of one another. Those among you who ally themselves with these belong with them. God does not guide transgressors."

From Verse 5:55: "Your real allies are God and His messenger, and the believers who observe the Contact Prayers (Sala), and give the obligatory charity (Zakat), and they bow down."

From Verse 18:102: "Do the Unbelievers think that they can take My Servants as protectors besides Me? Verily,

We have prepared Hell for the Unbelievers for (their) entertainment."

From Verse 18:106: "That is their reward, Hell, because they rejected faith, and took My Signs and My Messengers (that includes Muhammad) by way of jest."

From Verse 5:59: "Say, 'O people of the scripture (that means Christians and Jews), do you not hate us because we believe in God, and in what was revealed to us, and in what was revealed before us, and because most of you are not righteous?'"

From Verse 5:60: "Say, 'Let me tell you who are worse in the sight of God: Those who are condemned by God after incurring His wrath until He made them (as despicable) as monkeys and pigs, and the idol worshipers.'"

Does all of this sound remotely tolerant? Is this respectful of the Freedom of Religion guaranteed to all of us under the United States Constitution? Can these commands be compared, or indeed equaled, to Christianity's message of love? Is there any place in the New Testament where we are commanded to act with violence, like the Muslims are, toward non-believers?

## 6) THE KORAN ON THE TREATMENT OF INFIDELS

From Verse 9:3: "A proclamation is herein issued from God and His Messenger to all the people on the great day of pilgrimage, that God has disowned the idol worshipers, and so did His messenger (that means Muhammad). Thus, if you repent, it would be better for you. But if you turn away, then know that you can never escape from God. Promise those who disbelieve, a painful retribution."

From Verse 9:5: "Once the Sacred Months are past (and they refuse to make peace), you may kill the idol worshippers when you encounter them, punish them, and resist every move they make. If they repent and observe the Contact Prayers

(Salat) and give the obligatory charity (Zakat), you shall let them go. God is Forgiver, Most Merciful."

From Verse 9:13: "Would you not fight people who violated their treaties (to convert to Islam), tried to banish the messenger, and they are the ones who started the war in the first place? Are you afraid of them? God is the One you are supposed to fear, if you are believers."

From Verse 9:14: "You shall fight them, for God will punish them at your hands, humiliate them, grant you victory over them, and cool the chests of the believers."

From Verse 9:29: "You shall fight back against those who do not believe in God, nor in the Last Day, nor do they prohibit what God and His messenger have prohibited, nor do they abide by the religion of truth among those who received the scripture (note: that means Jews and Christians) until they pay the tax, willingly or unwillingly."

From Verse 9:111: "God has bought from the believers their lives and their money in exchange for Paradise. Thus, they fight in the cause of God, willing to kill and get killed."

Note: Notice here how in Christianity it is the blood of Jesus spilled for us, with nothing asked of us in exchange, that secures us paradise. In Islam, there is an exchange.

These are the mildest interpretations of the Koran I have seen. Other interpretations in fact say that those who do not pay the Zakat (Islamic tax) are to be put to death.

From the Sahih Muslim, book 019, Number 4294, Hadith:

Note: This is a quotation from the Prophet Muhammad.

"When you meet your enemies who are polytheists, invite them to three courses of action. If they respond to any one of these, you also accept and withhold yourself from doing them any harm. Invite them to accept Islam; if they respond to you, accept it from them and desist from fighting against them.... If they refuse to accept Islam, demand from them the Jizya

(Islamic tax). If they agree to pay, accept it from them and hold off your hands. If they refuse to pay the tax, seek Allah's help and fight them."

## 7) THE KORAN ON WOMEN

Sura 4, which was the 92nd verse written and therefore of prime importance, is one of the main Suras on women.

> From Verse 4:3: "If ye fear ye shall not be just toward orphans, marry women whom ye like—two at a time, or three or four; then if you fear you cannot keep two women equally, then marry only one or the bondwoman (i.e., a slave woman) that you own, this is closer to your not doing injustice."

Note some interesting concepts here: Polygamy is blessed in the name of doing justice to orphaned children, the slavery of women is implicitly approved of, and all this is done under the umbrella of men "not doing an injustice."

> From Verse 4:15: "If any of your women are guilty of lewd-ness, take the evidence of four reliable witnesses from among them; and if they testify, confine them to houses until death do claim them, or Allah ordain for them some other way."

Note: Does this mean that in cases of female lewdness (adultery included), the testimony of four reliable witnesses (who are all probably male) is sufficient to put the woman away until she dies?

Incidentally, this verse is not to be confused with Sharia law which dictates that regarding the discovery of a woman caught in the act of adultery, death by stoning is mandated.

# CHAPTER SIX
# ORIGINAL INTENT

What have some of the eminent fathers of our Judeo-Christian culture and religion said about Islam over the centuries?

Let us begin with Saint Thomas Aquinas, in Summa Contra Gentiles, Book 1, Chapter 6:

"The case is clear in the case of Muhammad. He seduced the people by promises of carnal pleasure to which the concupiscence of flesh goads us. His teaching also contained precepts that were in conformity with his promises, and gave free reign to carnal pleasures. In all this, as is not unexpected, he was obeyed by carnal men."

Further: "On the contrary Muhammad said that he was sent in the power of his Arms, which are signs not lacking even to robbers and tyrants. What is more, no wise men, men trained in things divine and human, believed in him from the beginning. Those who believe in him were brutal men and desert wanderers, utterly ignorant of divine teaching, through whose numbers Muhammad forced others to become his followers by the violence of his arms. Nor do divine pronouncements on the part of preceding prophets offer him any witness. It was therefore a shrewd decision on his part to forbid his followers to read the Old and the New Testaments, lest these books convict him of falsity."

Sir Winston Churchill, *The River War,* First Edition, Vol,. II, pages 248-250, London:

"How dreadful are the curses which Muhammadanism lays on its votaries! Besides the fanatical frenzy, which is as dangerous in a man as hydrophobia is in a dog, there is this fearful fatalistic apathy. The effects are apparent in many countries. Improvident habits, slovenly systems of agriculture, sluggish methods of commerce, and insecurity of property exist wherever the followers of the Prophet rule or live. A degraded sensualism deprives their life of its grace and refinement; the next of its dignity and sanctity. The fact that in Muhammadan law every woman must belong to some man as his absolute property, either as a child, a wife, or a concubine, must delay the final extinction of slavery until the faith of Islam has ceased to be a great power among men. Individual Moslems may show splendid qualities, but the influence of the religion paralyzes the social development of those who follow it. No stronger retrograde force exists in the world."

When referring to Muhammad, John Quincy Adams, America's sixth President (1824-1829), said the following:

"He poisoned the sources of human felicity at the fountain, by degrading the condition of the female sex, and the allowance of polygamy; and he declared undistinguishing and exterminating war, as a part of his religion, against all the rest of mankind. The essence of his doctrine was violence and lust—to exalt the brutal over the spiritual part of human nature...." (www.en.wikiquote.org/wiki/John_Quincy_Adams)

In 1876, British Prime Minister William E. Gladstone said the following about the Ottoman Turks, whose Islamic empire had brought the Caliphate (spiritual center of Islam) from Baghdad to European soil at Constantinople, after the first Turkish atrocities against Orthodox Christians in Bulgaria:

"Let the Turks now carry away their abuses in the only manner, namely, by carrying off themselves. Their Zaptiehs and their Mudirs, their Bimbashis and their Yuzbashis, their Kaimakams and their Pashas, one and all, bag and baggage, shall, I hope, clear out from the province that they have desolated and profaned" (www.en.wikipedia.org/wiki/William_Ewart_Gladstone).

George Horton, eminent U.S. diplomat and Consul General of the United States to Smyrna (modern-day Izmir in Turkey) spent thirty years in the Ottoman Empire and the Middle East. In a report to the U.S. Secretary of State on September 27, 1922, he said the following:

"The Mussulman religion, which is now having a great renaissance throughout the world, with its polygamy, its attitude toward women and to all non-Mussulman races, and the example and teachings of Muhammad as opposed to the teachings and life of Christ, is one of the dark forces at work in the world which are combining to destroy modern civilization."

Further, referring to the systematic extermination of Christian populations under the Islamic regime of the Ottoman Empire, Horton said:

"After the atrocious and frightful massacre of Armenians in 1915 of which I reported to the Department full accounts given me by native-born American eyewitnesses, representatives of American firms who came to Smyrna, I did not see how anyone could any longer have faith in the kindly intention of the Turks towards the Christian populations of the empire. About one million and a quarter Armenians perished in that awful affair, done to death by slow torture under circumstances of the most dreadful cruelty. This methodical extermination of the Christian population has been going on steadily ever since" (www.atour.com/~history/GG/20080717a.html).

## WHAT EMINENT U.S. JURISTS HAVE SAID

Let us now turn our attention to some landmark legal cases where the most eminent jurists, who were also among the Fathers of our Nation, and their successors, interpreted the legal framework they meant to establish with the U.S. Constitution and the First Amendment.

David Barton, in his detailed and truly excellent book titled, *Original Intent,* gives a number of such landmark cases. Let us begin with U.S. Supreme Court Justice James Iredell, who was nominated to the Court by President Washington. Justice Iredell wrote:

> "But it is objected that the people of America may perhaps choose representatives who have no religion at all, and that pagans and Mahometans (the expression used at the time for Muslims) may be admitted into offices . . . But it is never to be supposed that the people of America will trust their dearest rights to persons who have no religion at all, or a religion materially different from their own."

It is to be hoped that Justice Iredell's supposition that the people of America will never trust their rights to those who adhere to a religion materially different from their own will yet hold true.

John Adams wrote to Thomas Jefferson:

> "The general principles on which the fathers achieved independence were . . . the general principles of Christianity . . . Now I will avow that I then believed, and now believe, that those general principles of Christianity are as eternal and immutable as the existence and attributes of God . . . I could therefore safely say, consistently with all my then and present information, that I believed they would never make discoveries in contradiction to those general principles."

When the First Amendment was adopted, it is interesting to study what the underlying rationale and concerns were. Justice Story of the U.S. Supreme Court wrote at the time in his commentaries:

> "The real object of the First Amendment was not to countenance, much less to advance, Muhammadanism, or Judaism, or infidelity, by prostrating Christianity, but to exclude all rivalry among Christian sects," i.e., to ensure that no one

Christian sect overruled the other Christian sects. Justice Story (1779-1845), was the son of one of the original Boston Tea Party "Indians," was the Founder of the Harvard Law School, and was nominated to the Supreme Court by President James Madison.

George Mason, a member of the Constitutional Convention and the father of the Bill of Rights, wrote:

"All men have an equal, natural and inalienable right to the free exercise of religion, according to the dictates of conscience; and that no particular sect or society of Christians ought to be favored or established by law in preference to others."

In The People vs. Ruggles, 1811, Supreme Court of New York Chief Justice James Kent (one of the two acknowledged fathers of American jurisprudence) wrote:

"The free, equal and undisturbed enjoyment of religious opinion, whatever it may be, and free and decent discussions on any religious subject, is granted and secured; but to revile . . . the religion professed by almost the whole community is an abuse of that right . . . We are a Christian people and the morality of the country is deeply engrafted upon Christianity and not upon the doctrines or worship of those impostors (i.e. other religions)...."

In Vidal vs. Girard's Executors, 1844, U.S. Supreme Court, the great Daniel Webster, arguing for the plaintiff said:

"The plan of education proposed is anti-Christian and therefore repugnant to the law...."

Justice Story wrote:

"Christianity is not to be maliciously and openly reviled and blasphemed against, to the annoyance of believers or the injury of the public . . . Such a case is not to be presumed to exist in a Christian country."

In Church of the Holy Trinity vs. United States, 1892, in the U.S. Supreme Court, the Court stated:

"No purpose of action against religion can be imputed to any legislation, State or national, because this is a religious people . . . This is a Christian nation."

The definitions and principles laid down by William Blackstone in his *Commentaries on the Laws*, published in 1766, were used in yet another case Updegraph vs. The Commonwealth, 1824, in the Supreme Court of Pennsylvania, as follows:

"Blasphemy against the Almighty is denying His being or Providence or uttering contumelious (i.e., insulting) reproaches on our Savior Christ. It is punished as common law by fine and imprisonment, for Christianity is part of the laws of this land."

Contrast the above cases, decided by some of the Fathers of this Nation, to Mr. Obama's statement in 2007, and again in Turkey in June 2009, that America is not a Christian nation. On whose authority does he say such things? And why are Americans silent?

Let us close this section on legal precedent by stating that the requirement to declare a belief in God in order to hold public office was only struck down by the U.S. Supreme Court in 1961 in Torcaso vs. Watkins. That case and the 1947 Everson case in the U.S. Supreme Court, were the beginning of the judicial undoing of Christianity in America. In the Everson case, the Supreme Court, for the first time, spoke of the "wall between church and state." Surprisingly, these words and principles were not part of the Founding Fathers' language. Worse was to follow. History shows us that when a people cut themselves off from their spiritual and ethical roots, they become leaves in the wind and easy prey to conquest and spiritual degradation. This is where we are today—easy prey to Islamic propaganda because we have allowed our Judeo-Christian roots to be severed.

# CHAPTER SEVEN
# ISLAM IN AMERICA TODAY

We shall begin with the United States vs. Holy Land Foundation case, tried in November 2008 in the U.S. District Court for the Northeastern District of Texas, Dallas Division. The case number is CR NO. 3:04-CR-240-G (see page 125). Charges were brought against the Holy Land Foundation for raising, under false pretenses, $12 million in America which was then funneled to Hamas in the Middle East. Hamas is classified by the U.S. Government as a terrorist organization. The Defendants (Holy Land Foundation et al) were found guilty. Significantly, the judge found 302 Muslim civic organizations operating in the U.S. to be unindicted co-conspirators with Hamas, and ordered their names to be published. The list includes the largest Muslim civic organizations in America, the same organizations that both the Clinton and Bush administrations mistakenly treated as supposedly law-abiding and patriotic American organizations.

It transpires that most, if not all of them, are fronts for the Muslim Brotherhood, an organization bent on imposing Islam and Sharia law all over the world. Many unsuspecting contributors, even in America, have been giving them the funds with which to accomplish this.

The U.S. Government also introduced into evidence the archives of the Muslim Brotherhood in the U.S.A., which had been discovered by the FBI in 2004 in a sub-basement of a home in Annandale, Virginia belonging to Mr. Ismail Elbarasse, an MB member.

The defendant, the Holy Land Foundation, did not challenge the authenticity of those files, but merely motioned the Court to have them kept confidential. The judge rejected that Motion and instead ordered them published.

Among the files presented in evidence was an "Explanatory Memorandum On the General Strategic Goal for the Group in North America" dated May 22, 1991 (see Appendix 3), and authored by Mr. Mohamed Akram, an MB member. The Memorandum states in part:

> "The general strategic goal of the Group in America which was approved by the Shura Council and the Organizational Conference for the year (1987) is entitled 'Enablement of Islam in North America,' meaning: establishing an effective and a stable Islamic Movement led by the Muslim Brotherhood which adopts Muslims' causes domestically and globally, and which works to expand the Muslim base, aims at unifying and direct- ing Muslims' efforts, presents Islam as a civilization alternative, and supports the global Islamic State wherever it is."

"Islam as a civilization alternative" sounds like an effort to abro- gate U.S. democratic institutions and freedom of religion.

On page 4, paragraph 4, the Memorandum states:

> "The process of settlement is a 'Civilization-Jihadist Process' with all the word means. The Ikhwan (i.e., the MB member community) must understand that their work in America is a kind of grand jihad in eliminating and destroying the Western civilization from within and "sabotaging" its miserable house by the hands of the believers so that it is eliminated and God's religion is made victorious over all religions."

The Memorandum goes on in its Attachment 1, with a "List of our organizations and the organizations of OUR (capitals are mine) friends" (see Appendix 4). On that list are included twenty-nine of the largest civic Muslim-American organizations, such as ISNA (The Islamic Society of North America), MSA (The Muslim Students' Association), IMA (the Islamic Medical Association), MBA (the

Muslim Businessmen's Association), MYNA (the Muslim Youth of North America), NAIT (the North American Islamic Trust), AMSE (The Association of Muslim Scientists and Engineers), and many others. The largest of these "civic" organizations are the same ones that the Bush Administration reached out to in the period after 9/11, in an effort to show that it had dialogue with supposedly patriotic Muslim-American groups! Appendix 3 presents a copy of the full Memorandum (www.investigativeproject.org/documents/misc/20.pdf).

Why is the brief historical review of interest? It is because the House of Saud gained control of Arabia by the ruthless use of arms, because it has no true origin in Mecca or Medina, and because with its enormous wealth it is today hijacking Islam much as it did the holy cities of the Arabian peninsula.

As Professor Durre Ahmed of Pakistan has pointed out, Wahhabism is not the original form of Islam but rather a "moneytheist" form which has gained prominence because of money.

It is that same money that members of the Saudi royal family apparently use today to foment terrorism and the undermining of American and western European political and cultural institutions. As we have seen previously in this book, there are eyewitness accounts of such uses of Saudi money. Kamal Saleem, a former PLO terrorist who converted to Christianity, testifies to this in his book, *The Blood Of Lambs*.

Let us also look at examples of what is being taught to Muslim children and people going to mosques in America. At the Islamic Center in Oakland, California, I quote from the English High School text:

> "To be true Muslims, we must prepare and be ready for jihad in Allah's way. It is the duty of the citizen and the government. The military education is glued to the faith and its meaning and the duty to follow it."

The following is another quote taken from Islamic material apparently distributed to mosques in the U.S.:

"Muslims should work to form a society that is committed to the Islamic way of thinking and Islamic way of life, which means to form a government that implements principles of justice embodied in the Sharia...."

From the speech of Ihsan Bagby, Advisory Board member of ISNA (Islamic Society of North America) conference in August 2008 in Columbus, Ohio:

"We (Muslims) can never be full citizens of this country . . . because there is no way we can be fully committed to the institutions and ideologies of this country."

Didn't Major Hasan Nidal feel exactly the same way before he went on his killing rampage at Fort Hood?

At the same conference, Mr. Hatem Bazian from the Berkeley Islamic Studies program stated:

"It's about time that we have an intifada in this country that changes fundamentally the political dynamics in here."

From the Islamic Society of Greater Houston:

"So support for democracy is among those things that 'nullify one's Islam.'"

In September 2010, Sheikh Kifah Mustapha was escorted with a small group of special visitors on a guided tour through the FBI's National Counterterrorism Center and other secure government facilties, including the FBI's training center in Quantico, Virginia. This is part of the FBI's "outreach" program to the Muslim community. The problem is that Mr. Mustapha allegedly has extensive terrorist ties and supports Hamas. He was formerly employed by the Holy Land Foundation, the defendant in the Federal Court case in Texas cited earlier in this book. He was personally named as an unindicted co-conspirator in that case, and the prosecution presented evidence that he had been paid a total of $154,000 for his work for the Holy Land Foundation between 1996 and 2000.

During the trial, FBI Agent Lara Burns testified that Mr. Mustapha sang in a band sponsored by the HLF that regularly sang songs calling for the murder of Jews. Mr. Mustapha was also the registered agent for the Holy Land Foundation in Illinois and had trained as a Chaplain for the Illinois State Police. When the State Police withdrew Mustapha's appointment because of his documented support for terrorists, he brought suit against the Police for discrimination and was aided by CAIR, the Council on American Islamic Relations, another unindicted co-conspirator in the HLF case (see Appendix 5).

Now this same man is being escorted on a guided tour of America's most confidential domestic counter-terrorism facilities, and the nation's mainstream media fail to report any of this.

Let us now turn our attention to what some prominent, secular Muslims think, who are not classified as "militants" like Osama bin Laden. Below are some excerpts from an interview with General Hamid Gul, former chief of Pakistran's ISI (military intelligence services), conducted on September 26, 2001 by Arnaud de Borchgrave (www.upi.com/Top_news/Analysis/2010/07/282UP_interview_with_Hamid_Gul/UPI-60031280349846/).

**Question:** But you are against democracy, so how can there be a meeting of the minds?

**Answer:** Democracy does not work . . . The Koran says call a spade a spade. It is the supreme law and tells right from wrong . . . The creator's will predominates.

**Question:** So what kind of system are you advocating?

**Answer:** The world needs a post-modern system . . . The creator through Prophet Muhammad said equal distribution. Capitalism is the negation of the creator's will. It leads to imperialism and unilateralism.

**Question:** So what does this post-modern state system look like?

**Answer:** A global village under divine order, or we will have global bloodshed until good triumphs over evil. Islam encapsulates all the principal religions and what was handed down 1,400 years ago (i.e., the Koran) was the normal evolutionary sequel to Judaism and Christianity. The prophet's last sermon was a universal document of human rights for everyone that surpasses everything that came since, including America's Declaration of Independence and the U.N. Charter of Universal Rights. If you superimpose true secular values on true Islamic values, there is no difference. So surely divine law should supersede manmade law. Islam is egalitarian, tolerant, and progressive. It is the wave of the future.

What you have just read is supposed to be the secular, modern, and enlightened voice of Islam, spoken by a U.S. ally in Pakistan. It is a cry for the abolition of democracy in favor of an imposed theocratic regime. As Winston Churchill once observed, "Democracy is not a harlot to be picked up on the street corner, at the end of a Tommy gun."

Press any apologist for Islam, here or abroad, on this issue and sooner or later you will get to the same sort of statements. Who should our society believe: Winston Churchill, Saint Thomas Acquinas, John Quincy Adams, Thomas Jefferson, or General Hamid Gul and Feisal Abdul Rauf of the Ground Zero mosque?

# CHAPTER EIGHT

# THE OLD TESTAMENT AND THE NEW TESTAMENT

In the Old Testament (see Genesis 16), we learn that the Arab nation comes from Ishmael, the son of Abraham and the slave girl, Hagar. Ishmael was a son given by God to Abraham, but he was the result of a lack of faith. He was not the son of God's promise. God had promised the elderly Abraham a son with his wife Sarah, but the son did not come. So Abraham and Sarah, not sure if they trusted or fully understood God's prophecy, conspired for Abraham to lay with Sarah's slave girl, Hagar and Ishmael was conceived.

Genesis 16:11-12 tells us that the angel of the Lord told Hagar:

**"You are now with child and you will have a son. You shall name him Ishmael, for the Lord has heard of your misery.**

**"He will be a wild donkey of a man; his hand will be against everyone and everyone's hand against him, and he will live in hostility toward all his brothers"** (NIV).

Then God's prophecy was fulfilled and Sarah gave birth to Isaac. Hagar and Ishmael had to leave Abraham's household and went to settle in Egypt. There, we are told, Ishmael fathered the Arab nation. Let us note here that militant Islam is almost completely Arab-inspired and manned.

What does the New Testament tell us about all this? Let us go to Galatians 4:21-31 where the Apostle Paul tells us:

> Tell me, you who want to be under the law, are you not aware of what the law says?
>
> For it is written that Abraham had two sons, one by the slave woman and the other by the free woman.
>
> His son by the slave woman was born in the ordinary way; but his son by the free woman was born as a result of a promise.
>
> These things may be taken figuratively, for the women represent two covenants. One covenant is from Mount Sinai and bears children who are to be slaves: This is Hagar.
>
> Now Hagar stands for Mount Sinai in Arabia and corresponds to the present City of Jerusalem, because she is in slavery with her children.
>
> But the Jerusalem that is above is free, and she is our mother.
>
> For it is written: "Be glad, O barren woman, who bears no children; break forth and cry aloud, you who have no labor pains; because more are the children of the desolate woman than of her who has a husband."
>
> Now you, brothers, like Isaac, are children of promise.
>
> At that time the son born in the ordinary way persecuted the son born by the power of the Spirit. It is the same now.
>
> But what does the Scripture say? "Get rid of the slave woman and her son, for the slave woman's son will never share in the inheritance with the free woman's son."
>
> Therefore, brothers, we are not children of the slave woman, but of the free woman (NIV).

Note: at the time Saint Paul wrote Galatians in 49 A.D. from Antioch, Islam did not exist. It would not come into existence for another six hundred years, but Paul spiritually prepared Christians for it.

Let us also look at I John 4:3:

**And every spirit which does not acknowledge and confess that Jesus Christ has come in the flesh [but would annul, destroy, sever, disunite Him] is not of God [does not proceed from Him]. This [nonconfession] is the [spirit] of the antichrist, [of] which you heard that it was coming, and now it is already in the world"** (AMP).

As we set forth earlier in this book, in Sura 5:73 and in 5:75, the Koran teaches that Jesus was not God, but merely a messenger, and that God is not part of a Trinity as Christians believe.

Therefore, how reconcilable are the two religions on their theology? While it is true that other religions differ on their theology from Christianity and Judaism, none preach open violence against Christians and Jews like Islam does.

These are the facts.

# CHAPTER NINE

# THE ORIGINS OF ISLAMO-FASCISM IN THE MODERN ERA

## THE OTTOMAN EMPIRE AS CENTER OF THE CALIPHATE

In the late nineteenth and early twentieth centuries, the Ottoman Empire showed the full scope of how Islam treats infidels. Did the atrocities the Ottomans committed against the Christian minorities who had the misfortune of living under their regime begin in the late nineteenth century? Certainly not.

With the advent of worldwide journalism and fast communications, the atrocities came to the attention of the rest of the world. This chapter will not attempt to describe all the atrocities that the Ottoman Caliphate committed. However, what they did establish was an example for other Islamic regimes of what can be done to "infidel" minorities with impunity. Those lessons that they learned die hard. They will die one day, and the precedent of brutality and oppression that they set will be extinguished, but only if the rest of the world is finally willing to stand up and enforce its own principles.

In 1915, Constantinople was still the capital of the Ottoman Empire as well as the seat of the Caliphate. On March 10, 1915, the "Ottoman Fatwa" was issued. Allegedly, its author was Sheikh Shawish. The Fatwa provided the theological justification for the slaughter of more than two million Christians and the forcible evacuation out of Muslim-controlled lands of another million and a half Christians. To make an analogy, it would be as if the Vatican had issued a religious order to all Catholics, instructing and justifying the wholesale killing of non-Catholics all over the world.

The Fatwa begins by referring to Muslims who "have fallen under the rule of the infidels" and how these "oppressive infidels attack the center of the Caliphate...." It then commands:

"Today the holy war has become a sacred duty for every Muslim." Further it states, "They must know that the killing of the infidels who rule over the Islamic lands has become the sacred duty, whether it be secretly or openly, as the Koran declares in its words, 'Take them and kill them whenever you come across them, and we have given you a manifest power over them by revelation.'"

It also assaults non-Muslim laws on page 9 as follows:

"There can be absolutely no partnership in the native lands of Islam, for the rule of infidels over Muslims is not lawful, and it is not allowable that the Muslims should be judged by non-Muslims at any time whatever...."

What are the "native lands of Islam" according to this Fatwa? The answer is provided on page 11:

"India for the Muslim Indians, Java for the Muslim Javanese, Algeria for the Algerians among the Muslims, Morocco for the Moroccans, Tunis for the Muslim Tunisians, Egypt for the Muslim Egyptians, Iran for the Muslim Iranians, Turan for the Muslim Turanians, Bokhora for the Bokharians, Caucasus for the Caucasians, and the Ottoman kingdoms for the Muslim Turks and Arabia."

The Ottoman Fatwa is officially called "A Universal Proclamation To All The People Of Islam, The Seat of the Caliphate, 1333 (1915 A.D.) A full copy of it is published by the National Society of Defense. The English translation comes from the American Agency and

Consulate, Cairo, Egypt, in U.S. State Dept. document 867.4016/57, March 10, 1915.

Notice how even in countries with enormous non-Muslim populations like the Hindus in India, the Muslim minority is to rule and is called upon to kill the infidels. By what principle can 1.2 billion Hindus in India be ruled (and killed) by 130 million Muslims there?

What was the result of this Fatwa? To begin with, it provided the religious justification for slaughters of Christians that had already taken place in the Ottoman Empire:

- 30,000 Assyrian Christians killed in 1895

- 30,000 Bulgarian Christians killed in 1876

- 100,000 Armenian Christians killed in 1876

- 80 - 300,000 (depending on which historian one believes) killed in the Hamidian Massacres

- 7 - 11,000 Maronite Christians killed in Lebanon from 1842 - 1860

But worse, much worse was to come after the issuance of the Fatwa:

- 1,500,000 Armenian Christians killed between 1915-1920

- 200,000 Greek Christians killed in 1922 in Asia Minor

- 500,000 Greeks forcibly removed from Constantinople in September 1955. (They were, at least, not killed, but allowed to resettle in Greece.)

What was the crime of these poor people? Merely that they were Christians living under an Islamic regime which had provided the religious justification for their demise. They were, all along, treated as second-class citizens in the Ottoman Empire, forced to pay a special and onerous tax for not being Muslim. They were called "dhimma" and the principle behind this religious and financial discrimination is today known as "dhimmitude."

On December 28, 1895, in an article which appeared in *The New York Times*, British Prime Minister William E. Gladstone was quoted as follows:

"Still, Turks and other Mohammedans are not, so far as I know, plundered, ravished, murdered, starved, and burned; but this is the treatment that the Sultan knowingly deals out to his Armenian subjects daily. There are degrees in suffering, degrees in baseness and villainy among men, and both seem to have reached their climax in the case of Armenia."

Henry Morgenthau, who was subsequently to become one of Franklin D. Roosevelt's closest advisors, was serving as U.S. Ambassador to the Ottoman Empire from 1913 to 1916. In a telegram to the U.S. Secretary of State in 1915, he states in part: "Evidently Turkish nationalistic policy is aimed at all Christians and not confined to Armenians."

In an article he contributed to *The Red Cross Magazine*, in March 1918, Ambassador Morgenthau wrote:

"Will the outrageous terrorizing, the cruel torturing, the driving of women into the harems, the debauchery of innocent girls, the sale of many of them at eighty cents each, the murdering of hundreds of thousands, the deportation to and starvation in the deserts of other hundreds of thousands, the destruction of hundreds of villages and cities, will the willful execution of this whole devilish scheme to annihilate the Armenian, Greek and Syrian Christians of Turkey—will all this go unpunished?" (www.greek-genocide.org/quotes.html)

At the time, Ambassador Morgenthau called attention to the dangers of genocide. Very few listened in the U.S. Government. Less than thirty years later it was his misfortune, as well as the misfortune of the entire civilized world, to witness the genocide of his own people by the Nazis.

President Woodrow Wilson later acknowledged:

"I am in hearty sympathy with every just effort being made by the people of the United States to alleviate the terrible sufferings of the Greeks of Asia Minor. None have suffered more or more unjustly than they."

It is remarkable that President Wilson refers only to the efforts "of the people of the United States" and not to the U.S. Government, which did almost nothing. It is also remarkable that he does not refer to the sufferings of the Armenians at the hands of Islam. Their suffering, in fact, exceeded that of the Greeks. Many documentary books have been written about this genocide, and I highly recommend Peter Balakian's, *Black Dog of Fate* and *The Burning Tigris*.

The world community did not listen to Ambassador Morgenthau's warnings in 1915, and the genocide of Jews followed in World War II. The world community should wake up and remind itself now of what militant Islam has done through the centuries and be chastened for the future; otherwise, history may very well repeat itself.

## THE NAZI REGIME IN GERMANY

During World War II, the Grand Mufti of Jerusalem was one Amin Al-Husseini, a former officer in the Ottoman Army. With the fall of the last Sultan, Abdul Hamid II in 1909, and the imposition of the Turkish secular state under general Kemal Ataturk in 1920, the Caliphate had been removed from Constantinople. It has not been reestablished since, though Mecca has assumed the role of the spiritual center of Islam. During the 1940s, the Grand Mufti of Jerusalem had assumed the role of the spiritual leader of Islam.

On April 25, 1941, the Chief Mufti had been sent by the Nazis to occupied Bosnia, where he assumed the title of "Protector of Islam." The Nazis saw him as a useful leader. They hoped that he could foment rebellion within the camp of the Allies by inciting Muslims in British-held India, Egypt, and Palestine, Muslims in Dutch-held Java, and Muslims in other countries held by the Allies. Closer to home, the Nazis also hoped that the Chief Mufti would incite the Muslims in Bosnia to fight against the Catholic Croats and the Orthodox Serbs who were resisting Nazi occupation of their country with guerrilla warfare.

On November 28, 1941, the Grand Mufti paid a state visit to Adolf Hitler. Previously, Heinrich Himmler had also set up the ideological credentials of Islam by claiming that Muslims were of Aryan descent, and therefore acceptable to serve in the SS. Transcripts of the meeting with Hitler are easily available on the internet. The result of the meeting was the establishment of 13th Waffen SS Mountain Division, called the Hanjar Division. The Chief Mufti raised more than 20,000 Muslim men for this Division. Their senior commanders were German, while their officers were Muslim.

The flag of the Division was the Muslim scimitar (the handjar) over the swastika, and the men wore the Muslim fez when they were not wearing helmets. The Division became operational in March 1943 and was promptly sent into Croatia to extinguish Croat and Serb resistance to the Nazis, which was led by Marshal Tito (subsequent President of Yugoslavia). Depending on whose account one reads, this Division killed tens of thousands of civilians and resistance fighters in Serbia and Croatia, before being sent to France and then to Hungary. The Division finally surrendered to the British in Hungary on May 7, 1945.

At his meeting with Hitler, Mr. Al-Husseini had predicted that "the Almighty could never award the victory to an unjust cause," and in this prediction he was proven right. The Almighty saw through the injustice and brutality of both Hitler's and Mr. Al-Husseini's work, and awarded victory where it belonged—to the Allied cause.

## ISLAMO-FASCISM TODAY

We will not unnecessarily dwell on this subject here. Theocratic regimes such as the Islamic Republic of Iran, the Taliban government in Afghanistan (ended in 2001), and Saudi Arabia supply ample evidence of the worst kind of fascism—a fascism that is not only political but also immoral. Hideous capital punishment for infractions like theft, homosexuality, adultery, the complete enslavement of women, the sentencing in effect of fifty percent of the population to insignificance, and the prejudice against all infidels are hallmarks of these regimes.

Additionally, violence with potential mass destruction of life in the hands of nuclear-armed theocratic regimes is a very real danger.

By contrast, Western democracies have proven their mettle. In the period after World War II, when they had a monopoly on nuclear weapons, they did not resort to mass killings of Muslims. Can the same be said with certainty about the Islamic theocratic regimes today if they had had a monopoly on such weapons?

I do not think so.

There is no such thing as a radical Muslim and a moderate Muslim. There are, rather, only Muslims who abide by the Koran literally, and those who ignore it. However, there is no doubt that on the theology, on what Islam really preaches, the so-called jihadists are right, and the moderates are wrong.

Kamal Saleem, a former PLO terrorist who came to the U.S. in 1981 with Saudi money to subvert the country and then converted to Christianity in 1985, draws in his recent book titled, *The Blood Of Lambs*, a stark comparison. He talks of Islam as "a message of power, discipline, and success" and he refers to Christianity as the message of love. He also talks about how cut off and alone Islam left him, of how he had "many brothers in jihad, but no friends." Referring to his conversion to Christianity, he says:

> "Through the hands of the innocent, a force washed over me that I had not been trained to resist: love. This love was huge and overpowering, but it did not require of me my blood or my strength or my hatred. It required only my surrender."

What beautiful words, so true of the coming to Christ!

Religions, based on Judeo-Christian principles, are loving and tolerant. Islam is unrelenting and, in the hands of fundamentalist Muslims, fascist. Let us be ever mindful of how this religion treats its own people when given free rein. Let us also be mindful of the track record accumulated by this religion when given a chance.

# CHAPTER TEN

# CAN THE TWO RELIGIONS BE RECONCILED?

## DIFFERENT THEOLOGIES

On theology, the two religions are irreconcilable. The only way they can peacefully coexist is through forbearance—the forbearance of Christians in willfully overlooking the violent nature of strict Islam, and the forbearance of Muslims who are willing to overlook and not practice the bellicose mandates of Islam.

America has repeatedly proven its Judeo-Christian principles in its treatment of Muslims around the world. From untold millions spent in aid for flood victims in Pakistan, to tsunami victims in Indonesia, to removing Saddam Hussein from his conquest of Kuwait and the enslavement of Iraqis, America has always been there to help. Let us also not forget America's involvement in the Balkan Wars in the mid-1990s. It was on December 31, 1995 that the U.S. 1st Armored Division (nicknamed "Hell on Wheels") under the command of General William G. Boykin, crossed the Sava River into Bosnia-Herzegovina. They were there to finally offer effective protection to Muslims in Bosnia ("Bosniaks"). Only five months before the arrival of the American Army and while under the theoretical protection of Dutch troops, eight thousand Bosniaks had been summarily executed by Serbian forces in the town of Srebernica. The American Forces stopped all that. They then became the nucleus of a joint NATO-United Nations Stabilization Force (SFOR), which went on to track down and arrest war criminals like Goran Jelisic and turn them over to the International Court of Justice at the Hague.

And yet, while America keeps on giving proof of its humanity and support for Muslims, what happens? It is labeled a "crusader," and its patriotic generals are denounced by the Islamic radicals and those who have been deceived by their over-devotion to political-correctness.

All the while, as America keeps doing what is right, what do the forces of radical Islam do?

Let us look briefly at the story of Mr. Abdurahman Alamoudi.

Mr. Alamoudi was born in Eritrea and became a U.S. citizen in 1979. After emigrating to the U.S., he became quite rich quickly. He also was selected by the U.S. State Department as a Goodwill Ambassador (much like Feisal Rauf was recently). He worked with the U.S. Department of Education, was repeatedly received and photographed with Karl Rove and Presidents Clinton and Bush, and was welcomed on Capitol Hill.

During the 2000 Presidential Campaign season, he made at least two $10,000 contributions to establish the Islamic Institute. He was viewed as a "moderate Muslim" and the *Washington Post* described him as "a pillar of the local Muslim community."

During his years as a "pillar," he founded two dozen prominent Muslim organizations in America, including the American Muslim Armed Forces and Veterans Affair Council. He also founded the Muslim Chaplain Program of the Armed Forces.

Then in the fall of 2003, Mr. Alamoudi was arrested by the Scotland Yard at Heathrow Airport carrying a suitcase with $340,000 in cash. When asked where he had found this money, he apparently replied that he had opened his hotel room door that morning and found the suitcase waiting outside. Upon investigation, it was established that he had just returned from Libya. He is now serving a twenty-three year sentence in federal prison. It turns out that he was an Al-Qaeda "financier." Apparently, he had funneled more than $1 million to Al-Qaeda.

So who can be trusted? Will the American Muslim community effectively police itself and clean itself up, before demanding recognition from the rest of the citizens of America? Why won't America's Muslims demand the withdrawal of the hate-filled books used in their schools? Why will they not put an end to the jihadi rhetoric of most of their sermons and expel the fiery imams? How wonderful would it be if the Muslim communities in America were to produce another Martin Luther King instead of yet another jihadi.

## THE DIFFERING HISTORY OF IMMIGRANTS WHO CAME TO AMERICA

Waves of immigration have made America great—pilgrims from England, Germany, Sweden, Italy, Greece, Ireland, and the slaves brutally brought to America from West Africa against all Christian and human rights principles. They all assimilated and contributed to the greatness of America today and taught everyone how America is the miracle of modern times, the country where humanity comes first. The Revolutionary War that started in 1776 was fought with Protestants, Catholics, and Jews fighting alongside each other. One of George Washington's top battlefield officers was General Sullivan, and one of his top staff officers was Lt. Colonel Isaac Franks. Haym Solomon, a Jewish businessman in Philadelphia, gave up his considerable fortune to finance Washington's Army in the difficult winter of 1776 - 1777. He personally borrowed $50,000 with which to pay for supplies and wages for the Continental Army, prior to its crossing the Delaware on Christmas Eve 1776. He died holding $636,000 of debt from the Continental Congress. He was never repaid a penny.

Other Jews in America, such as Mathias Bush, Aaron Solomon, Francis Salvador, and Aaron Lopez gave up everything for the American cause. In gratitude for Haym Solomon's sacrifices, President Washington asked him by what means he wished to be honored by the new republic. His answer was to ask that on the new one dollar bill, the image over the great seal of the President, which represented the thirteen original colonies, be shaped in the form of the Star of David. That symbol is still on the dollar bill today.

A Catholic Frenchman, Pierre Caron de Beaumarchais, who wrote two operas, *The Barber Of Seville* and *The Marriage of Figaro*, was another patriot. He also lost his fortune and died a pauper, after the U.S. Government failed to repay him for the several shiploads of supplies and ammunition that he had purchased in France to help the War of Independence. A Prussian army officer, Baron von Steuben, trained Washington's ragtag army into a fighting force effective enough to defeat the British Imperial army. He too died an early and impoverished death.

These are the examples that truly represent "being part of America's story from the beginning," and not what President Obama had in mind when he made his Cairo speech.

Where are the American heroes of Muslim background? Heroes whose stories can parallel the stories we have described above? Where are they even today?

Why will so many of the Muslims in America not follow the example of all these immigrants? Why will so many of them not assimilate? What is it that holds them back? Is it because of what Islam teaches? When will they begin to clean up their own communities from the killers such as the Major Hassans, the Alamoudis, the Christmas Day bombers, the New Year's Day bombers, and all the rest who poison the well?

Can we be satisfied to hear vague reassurances from the Muslim communities in America and in Europe who say: "Well, the majority of us do not agree with the jihadists?" What about the minority? And what damage can that minority do?

# CHAPTER ELEVEN
# WHAT CAN BE DONE?

Hope for Europe and America lies in the following:

a) facing militant Islam with force: political, military, spiritual, and legal. By legal we mean actually changing the laws of Western countries to take account of the particular and militant characteristics of Islam (see section on the Shinto Directive below).

b) praying that the good Lord will bring Muslims revelation through His Holy Spirit.

c) the continuing awakening of Muslim women whose destiny under Islam is not freedom and equality, as Mr. Feisal Abdul Rauf falsely claims, but insignificance and injustice. We regularly read of the oppressed in Islam, whose only solution is to set themselves on fire and die (see article in *The New York Times*, November 8, 2010).

d) changing the laws so that freedom of religion is not accorded to a violent and retrograde system of life, as the U.S. Treasury Department Paper No. 4 confirms (see Chapter Two). Remember that Islam is a "whole-life system." It is not just a religion.

e) demanding symmetry in relations with theocratic regimes. Building a mosque in New York which would in any way be connected with a theocratic regime like Iran's or Saudi Arabia's should be based on the right to build and safely operate churches of other faiths in those theocratic countries.

f) enforcing the United Nations' Universal Declaration of Human Rights (UDHR).

There should be an equivalent of the U.N. International Atomic Energy Agency established, to be called the Human Rights Enforcement Agency, or similar. Its mission should be to bring before the General Assembly, first for reprimand but eventually for expulsion, any regime which violates the U.N.'s Universal Declaration of Human Rights (UDHR).

Sadly, today we have a situation where those who patently violate the UDHR have been moralizing to the rest of us. Words have lost their meaning at the U.N. and, what is worse, the ethical principles of mankind have lost their meaning.

Return the United Nations to what its lofty founding principles were rather than the aberrant influence we see exercised over it by the fifty-six nation Organization of Islamic Conference.

Does this sound simplistic or impossible? It is not. The right of freedom of religion must be based on that same right being extended back to the other major religions of the world. Violence or the threat of violence should not be any part of the formula. Governments should come up with the corresponding laws, as they did when the Potsdam Declaration and the Shinto Directive were promulgated in 1945. The United Nations should be obliged to be true to its mission, rather than the misleading parroting it now engages in.

## THE SHINTO DIRECTIVE

There is a convincing precedent from modern times of the same type of conflict we are now experiencing with radical Islam, and how it was dealt with.

In World War II, the Allies were forced to deal with another "whole-life" system, similar to Islam, namely the Shinto culture in Japan. Shinto called for many practices that were alien to Western principles, including Bushido and the Samurai warrior code. It was a theology, mixed into a war-like feudal system, where respect for basic human life and rights were not present. Shinto theology also held that the god, Amaterasu, had willed that the people of Japan were superior to other people. Can we see any parallels with the mandates of militant Islam here?

When General Douglas MacArthur became Supreme Allied Commander in Japan in August 1945, he implemented laws to separate religion in Japan from the rest of the Shinto way of life. The result was the so called Shinto Directive, promulgated by the Supreme Commander for the Allied Powers to Japan on December 15, 1945 (see Appendix 6).

Before analyzing the Shinto Directive mandates, let us briefly focus on its moral precedent, the Potsdam Declaration of July 26, 1945. The Potsdam Declaration was signed prior to the end of the war in the Pacific by President Harry S. Truman, Prime Minister Clement Attlee of the United Kingdom (Prime Minister Winston Churchill had just finished negotiating the Declaration when his party lost the elections), and Generalissimo Chiang Kai-Shek of China. It contained thirteen Articles.

Article 4 reads: "The time has come for Japan to decide whether she will continue to be controlled by those self-willed militaristic advisers whose unintelligent calculations have brought the Empire of Japan to the threshold of annihilation, or whether she will follow the path of reason."

Article 6 reads: "There must be eliminated for all time the authority and influence of those who have deceived and misled the people of Japan into embarking on world conquest—for we insist that a new order of peace, security, and justice will be impossible until irresponsible militarism is driven from the world."

Article 10 reads: "We do not intend that the Japanese shall be enslaved as a race or destroyed as a nation, but stern justice shall be meted out to all war criminals, including those who have visited cruelties upon our prisoners. The Japanese government shall remove all obstacles to the revival and strengthening of democratic tendencies among the Japanese people. Freedom of speech, of religion, and of thought, as well as respect for fundamental human rights, shall be established."

Does this sound similar to the challenge of Islam, the Koran, and Sharia?

The Shinto Directive took the moral principles enumerated in the Potsdam Declaration and implemented them. Article 1 of the Directive states:

"In order to prevent a recurrence of the perversion of Shinto theory and beliefs into militaristic and ultra-national-istic propaganda designed to delude the Japanese people and lead them into wars of aggression, and in order to assist the Japanese people in a dedication of their national life to build-ing a new Japan based upon ideals of perpetual peace and democracy...."

Article 1a of the Directive states:

"The sponsorship, support, perpetuation, control, and dissemination of Shinto by the Japanese national, prefectural and local governments, or by public officials, subordinates, and employees acting in their official capacity are prohibited and will cease immediately."

We will leave the readers to reach their own conclusions on the parallels here. Suffice it to say, since 1945, Japan has enjoyed unprecedented freedom, peace, and prosperity. It is fair to say that the country has never had a more happy existence, and the murderous bigotry that was used by its former leaders has been discredited.

We need a modern-day equivalent of the Shinto Directive for America and Europe—a new set of laws which will separate the the-ology of Islam from its militant political, financial, and all-conquering ideology. Islam can be protected as a religion in the West, but not as a whole-life system. Islamic preaching of violence in the mosques must at the very least be brought under the strict purvey and consequences of hate speech laws. Consideration should also be given to obliging Muslims who were born in the U.S.A. to give the Oath of Allegiance, which only immigrants taking U.S. citizenship now are obliged to do. Militant Muslims, like Major Nidal Hasan, should not be allowed to serve in the military. If the CIA can successfully monitor the patriotism of its employees, so should the U.S. Armed Forces.

## THE UNITED NATIONS

The Universal Declaration of Human Rights (UDHR) was formally adopted by the United Nations General Assembly in Paris on December 10, 1948. The UDHR has thirty simple and straightforward Articles. Since 1968, when the U.N. International Conference on Human Rights agreed that the UDHR constitutes an obligation for all members of the international community, Muslim states have been obliged to observe and practice these Articles (www.un.org/en/documents/udhr/index.shtml).

As we look at various theocratic and Islamic regimes, we can readily see that they are in violation of at least Articles 1, 2, 3, 4, 5, 8, 11, 14, 18, 19, 21, 22, 25, 26, 29, and 30 of the UDHR. Let us focus on only some of these Articles.

- Article 3: "Everyone has the right to life, liberty, and security of person."

- Article 5: "No one shall be subjected to torture or to cruel, inhuman, or degrading treatment or punishment."

- Article 8: "Everyone has the right to an effective remedy by the competent national tribunals for acts violating the fundamental rights granted him by the constitution or the law." Note: *Does the finality of stoning someone to death for homosexuality or adultery, or of cutting off a hand for theft, allow for an effective subsequent remedy by the competent national tribunals?*

79

- Article 11: "Everyone charged with a penal offense has the right to be presumed innocent until proved guilty...."

- Article 18: "Everyone has the right to freedom of thought, conscience, and religion; this right includes freedom to change religion or belief...." *What about the fatwas issued with impunity by Islamic regimes against those Muslims who have converted to other religions—the same regimes that then come into the United Nations General Assembly and moralize to other nations?*

- Article 19: "Everyone has the right to freedom of opinion and expression; this right includes freedom to hold opinions without interference and to seek, receive, and impart information and ideas through any media and regardless of frontiers."

- Article 21 (3): "The will of the people shall be the basis of the authority of government; this will be expressed in periodic and genuine elections which shall be by universal and equal suffrage and shall be held by secret vote or by equivalent free voting procedures."

- Article 22: "Everyone . . . is entitled . . . to the free development of his personality."

- Article 26 (2): "Education shall be directed to the full development of the human personality and to the strengthening of respect for human rights and fundamental freedoms."

- Article 30: "Nothing in this Declaration may be interpreted as implying for any State, group, or person any right to engage in any activity or to perform any act aimed at the destruction of any of the rights and freedoms set forth herein."

Additionally, in 1952, the U.N. General Assembly adopted the Convention on the Political Rights of Women. In 1979, the U.N. also adopted the Convention on the Elimination of All Forms of Discrimination Against Women. In November 1981, the U.N. General Assembly adopted and proclaimed the declaration on the Elimination of All Forms of Intolerance and of Discrimination Based on Religion or Belief. Has anyone bothered to raise the question of the rights of women or of the rights of non-Muslims (preaching, having houses of worship, etc.) in many of the Islamic countries? There are, therefore, five Conventions in all that the United Nations has adopted regarding the equality of women and the freedom of religion. All of them are being systenatically violated by Islamic countries.

What has happened here? Is the United Nations true to its mission statement, and its members true to the undertakings they made in order to join, or is it the modern day equivalent of the Tower of Babel?

When will the U.N. enforce its own rules and expel those who do not recognize and observe them and who, instead, also have the temerity to lecture the rest of the free nations? When will such nations be held up to public opprobrium?

## THE ORGANIZATION OF ISLAMIC CONFERENCE (OIC)

This Organization was founded on September 25, 1969 and numbers fifty-seven Muslim nations. Currently, its Secretary General is Professor Ekmeleddin Ihsanoglu of Turkey. It tends to act as a voting bloc within the United Nations, thus geometrically enlarging the importance of the Islamic bloc in negotiations within the U.N. on proposed Resolutions of the General Assembly.

But what does the OIC Charter say?

In Chapter 1 (Objectives and Principles) Article 1, paragraph 7:

"To reaffirm its support for the rights of peoples as stipulated in the U.N. Charter and international law."

Have we not already seen that the U.N. Charter calls for observance by its Members of the decisions of the General Assembly of the U.N. (including the Universal Declaration of Human Rights adopted by the U.N. in 1948), and that at least five of those decisions, adopted in 1948, 1952, 1968, 1979, and 1981 have to do with equal rights for women and with freedom of religion and freedom to exit a religion?

As we read on in the OIC Charter, Chapter 1 (Objectives and Principles), Article 1, paragraph 14:

"To promote and to protect human rights and fundamental freedoms including the rights of women, children, youth, elderly, and people with special needs as well as the preservation of Islamic family values." Doesn't it say: "Fundamental freedoms" and "rights of women?" Have words in the English language completely lost their meaning in the face of unrelenting Islamic propaganda?

Going back to the U.N. Charter, Chapter 1, Article 1, paragraph 3, we read:

"To achieve international cooperation in solving international problems of an economic, social, cultural, or humanitarian character, and in promoting and encouraging respect for human rights and for fundamental freedoms for all without distinction as to race, sex, language, or religion."

If the OIC Charter obliges the OIC to support the U.N. Charter, which calls for freedom of religion and equal rights for women, is not the OIC in violation of its own charter? What fundamental freedoms do women enjoy under strict Islam, when the Koran views them as the source of sin because of Eve and then turns them into a subservient species?

On the subject of women let us ask: Can women vote in all the OIC member countries? Do they have equal property rights? Do they have equal marital rights with men in the marriage? Does the testimony of one woman equal the testimony of one man in court? Or do they observe what the Koran says, namely that the testimony of two women is necessary to oppose the testimony of one man?

How does the OIC police itself when its own members violate its charter?

Reading further from the OIC Charter:

Chapter 1, Article 1, paragraph 11: "To disseminate, promote and preserve the Islamic teachings and values based on moderation and tolerance, promote Islamic culture, and safeguard Islamic heritage."

Several questions come to mind here:

a) If part of the OIC mission is to promote Islamic teachings, which of themselves deny freedom of religion (remember Suras 5 and 9), equal rights for women etc. and, at the same time, the OIC Charter calls for upholding the U.N. Charter, is it not by definition contradictory?

b) Are there Christian or Jewish or Buddhist international-treaty associations which band together all the co-religionist nations of their religion, and whose publicly announced aim is to "disseminate and promote" Christian or Jewish or Buddhist teachings?

c) When organizations like the OIC demand that they be given the right to free religion and to disseminate their religion in Christian and other non-Muslim countries, do they simultaneously extend the same rights to other religions in their own countries? Should they not be forced to, at the penalty of losing their recognition by major world international collaborative bodies?

d) When this paragraph in the OIC Charter obliges their member countries to be "based on moderation and tolerance," do they really tolerate other religions like Christianity in their own countries?

I repeat: How does the OIC police itself, and why does the U.N. and other international bodies not refuse the OIC recognition when it is manifestly in violation of its own Charter?

Let us also focus on Chapter 2, Article 6 of the U.N. Charter. It reads:

"A Member of the United Nations which has persistently violated the Principles contained in the present Charter may be expelled from the Organization by the General Assembly upon the recommendations of the Security Council." How effective is the United Nations in policing itself and the adherence of its Members to its Charter?

Let us also contrast the lofty objectives put forward by the OIC with the pictures we have all seen of women accused of adultery and buried up to their necks in the ground, ready to be stoned to death. Can we remember that one of the women executed was the favorite granddaughter of Saudi Arabia's King Abdullah? This granddaughter had apparently been married off at a young age to a man selected for her. Her marriage was unhappy, and she entered a relationship with a young Saudi man whom she loved. They were apprehended in a coastal hotel outside Jeddah in the 1970s. She was executed by stoning on the palace grounds, which then Crown Prince Abdullah was forced to watch. Her lover was not, as I recall. The case had been widely reported by the BBC at the time. Remember, General Gul's statement to Arnaud de Borchgrave that Islam is "egalitarian, tolerant and progressive."

# CHAPTER TWELVE
# CONCLUSION

Crude oil has been the great enabler for radical Islam in the twentieth century. Crude oil lies at the top of the pyramid of evil. It has given radical Islam incredible riches with which to wreak havoc on the Judeo-Christian civilization, both secular and spiritual. In 2008 alone, the United States paid over $45 billion to Saudi Arabia. The twenty-two thousand madrassahs operating around the world with the support of Saudi money produce more than four million mostly radicalized young Muslim men every year. They know nothing of the New Testament. In fact, they are forbidden from even reading it. They also know nothing of the Torah, of Hinduism, Buddhism, or any other major religion of this world.

They do know to yearn for martyrdom and for the seventy-two virgins that they will each get to deflower in Jinnah, Islam's version of paradise.

As for the women of Islam: We must wonder what their paradise consists of.

Let us hope that the twenty-first century will bring a new awakening to us on the following ills that plague us:

1) Dependence on Middle Eastern energy sources.

2) Political correctness and extending religious freedom to those who are not willing to extend it to us. To make no finer point, our laws need to be changed to meet this challenge from militant Islam, because Islam does not play by our rules.

3) Spiritual complacency which has permitted the radicalized sons of Hagar and Ishmael to mount a civilization and religion challenge right on the home territory of Judeo-Christsian culture and civilization.

Militant Islam needs to be held up to public scrutiny. It needs, also, to be properly identified for what it is. The U.S. is not fighting a "war against terror," as the Bush Administration lamely defined it, nor a "war on extremism," as the Obama Administration laughingly labels it. The U.S. is in fact fighting a war against militant Islam. The first tenet of any war is to properly identify and label the enemy. Wars have no room for the type of political correctness, or willful disregard of mortal danger, which we have been witnessing for the last two decades.

America needs to wake up, and its leaders need to stop misleading the nation on the dangers it faces.

Ultimately, God's will shall be done. There will be end days. Too much prophecy in the Old and New Testaments confirm this. Muslim armies from countries like Russia, Azerbaijan, Kazakhstan, Turkey, Syria, Iran, Egypt, Sudan, Ethiopia, and Libya may well converge on Israel to destroy it. These armies, we are told in the Old Testament, will be destroyed. Some forecasts show that by the year 2025, substantial percentages (20 to 40 percent) of European nations' armies will be Muslim. Will they be loyal to the Western principles we all treasure?

Ezekiel 38 and 39 testify to the coming conflagration.

Revelation 2:12 tells us that the seat of Satan on earth is Pergamum, in modern-day Turkey. Turkey has already begun its shift away from being a secular Muslim state into an Islamic state. Its leadership is perhaps vying for re-establishment of the Caliphate in Turkey. A manifestation of this shift was, quite probably, the bloody incident on the M/V Mavi Marmara with the relief ship flotilla Turkey sent to Gaza in the Spring of 2010 in defiance of the Israeli and Egyptian blockade. The Turkish government's footprint was all over this supposedly private undertaking. A Turkish citizen is Secretary General of the Organization of Islamic Conference. And there are rumors that Turkey has recently signed a secret pact with Iran under which Turkey is recognized as the leader of Sunni Muslims, Iran is recognized as the leader of the Shia Muslims, and both countries commit to re-establishing the Caliphate.

Egypt and Turkey were already conspiring, under the Mubarak regime, to declare that they have a common sea border that is several hundred miles long. They were planning to declare all that sea space in the eastern Mediterranean an Exclusive Economic Zone, as defined in the United Nations. Convention of the Law of the Sea. That means that they would be able to control who exploits all natural resources. The trouble with their plan is that under the very same U.N. Convention of the Sea, Turkey and Egypt do not have a common sea border. They only get to claim they have one by ignoring the Convention's rules and the existence of a bunch of Greek islands which annoyingly stand in their way. What their plan represents, however, is a transparent effort to "Islamize" the eastern Mediterranean Sea. Any successor government to Mubarak's is likely to have heavy dependence on the Muslim Brotherhood, and to try and further advance this preposterous scheme.

Secular regimes in Islamic countries, including Tunisia, Yemen, Jordan, and now Egypt, are falling or under severe pressure. Behind the street opposition in those countries also lurks the Muslim Brotherhood. In Egypt, the MB had been fielding 20 percent of the popular votes in recent elections. We have seen a similar phenomenon develop in Turkey over the last fifteen years. Mr. Erdogan's Islamic party entered politics fielding a small minority of the popular vote, only to manage to win national elections with an absolute majority within ten years. Now Turkey is rapidly being converted from a secular state into an Islamic state. With Turkey's change of direction goes the second largest standing army in the European continent (after Russia's). Egypt is next, and with its change of direction goes the loss of safe transit through the Suez Canal, not to mention the possible loss of the Camp David Peace Accords between Israel and Egypt.

Stay tuned.

# EPILOGUE
# QUESTIONS STILL LEFT TO BE ANSWERED

As I complete this book, I am staying in Eretria, one of the best known ancient Greek city-states, in Evia, Greece. Waves of ambitious conquerors have washed over this place from ancient times: Persians, Muslim pirates from the Barbary Coast, Ottomans, Venetians, and most recently the Nazis. Herodotus mentions in his history how the whole city-state of Eretria was put to the torch in 480 B.C. by King Xerxes of Persia, after he overran King Leonidas and his three hundred Spartans at Thermopylae. Like all would-be conquerors of Greece, he too eventually came to failure and defeat by the Greeks. Shortly after burning Eretria, his fleet was destroyed by the Athenians at Salamis, to be followed by the complete destruction of his army by the Spartans at the Battle of Plateai in 479 B.C.

Untold blood has been spilled to keep these parts free. And yet, the would-be conquerors keep coming and the blood keeps flowing. Will that sort of history repeat itself here, only this time brought on by the new worldwide aggressor, radical Islam?

Distinguished linguists and Arabists in the West like Dr. Gunter Luling, Dr. Christoph Heger, and Thomas Milo have pointed out how the lack of knowledge of Arabic script and the possible alteration of the original texts of the Koran may have subverted or, indeed, altered what was actually written down during Muhammad's time. For example, there is evidence that punctuation marks have been introduced to the original Koranic texts, the effect of which is to alter the true meaning that Muhammad may have been trying to convey. You will recall that the Koran's verses were not actually all placed into a book of 114 verses until 650 A.D., by Caliph Othman. It has also been pointed out that there is strong evidence that at least two Koranic verses, 96 and 80, were substantively altered early on when the Islamic conquests began. See the following websites: www. abebooks.com/servlet/SearchResults?an=gunter+1%FCling&sts=t&x =0&y=0 and www.christoph-heger.de/Surah_74_30.htm

Western Koranic experts and linguists have also complained that each time an ancient and original version of the Koran emerges at auction, it is promptly snapped up into private collections, most probably by very wealthy Arabs. Thus, it is then no longer available for the kind of academic scrutiny it deserves. As a result, theories about alterations of the original Koranic scripts exist, and they remain unresolved.

Is it possible that, after the death of Muhammad in 632 A.D., his successors as Caliphs allowed or condoned such alterations, having already decided that conquest by force of arms was to be their plan? More importantly, is it possible that entire generations comprising hundreds of millions of Muslims have been schooled in an aggressive and bellicose Koran (recall Verses 5 and 9 in particular) that does not represent the true intention of Muhammad?

A definitive answer escapes us, though Muhammad's letter to the Byzantine Emperor Heraclius in 629 A.D. is quite telling.

Only with the opening of Islamic societies, and the courage to face truths, can such matters be explored. In the meantime, what is certain is that Saudi-financed "money-theism" combined with the Muslim Brotherhood, the Saudi regime's otherwise mortal enemy but effective ally in the worldwide struggle to impose Islam and Sharia law on all, is slowly but surely leading mankind back to the spilling of blood.

When will we all learn how to live in peace and really respect each other?

And when will we acknowledge that the Koran has already been interpreted, in the thirteen hundred and sixty years since it was written, by Islam's most prominent religious scholars? And that their interpretations all coincide and reconfirm the inferiority of women and the obligation of every Muslim to engage in worldwide conquest for Islam? We so often hear that the Koran is a poetic work, written in classical Arabic and that it is extremely difficult to interpret. And yet, the Koran has repeatedly been interpreted, and we can readily find those interpretations in books such as, *Reliance of the Traveller, Tafsir Ibn Kathir,* and others.

In addition to the interpretations of Islamic scholars, we have another body of evidence that shows how Muhammad's followers interpreted the Koran: The violent campaigns of conquest unleashed by Islam against Jerusalem, the Byzantine Empire, and Europe within just a few years after Muhammad's death. As we have seen earlier in this book, by 890 A.D. the forces of Islam had turned the Mediterranean Sea into an Islamic lake. Their record of conquest and violence is overwhelming and unparalleled in the annals of human history. This violence continued all the way to 1805 A.D., when the decisions of President Jefferson ended Islamic piracy and imposed peace in the Mediterranean Sea.

Is not all of this evidence enough?

Can we convincingly argue that Islam has renounced violence today?

Are we entitled to expect that the forces of moderates within Islam will stand against the forces of radicalism so that we can all enjoy God's creation in peace?

# APPENDIXES

1) Chronological List of the Suras of the Koran

2) Partial List of Mosques built over Christian and other Temples

3) "An Explanatory Memorandum" written by Mohamed Akram of the Muslim Brotherhood, May 22, 1991

4) List of Organizations that are Fronts for the Muslim Brotherhood

5) Attachment A from the Holy Land Foundation trial, November 2008, List of Unindicted Co-Conspirators

6) The Shinto Directive

# FURTHER READING SOURCES

1) *Original Intent*, by David Barton, August 2008, Wallbuilder Press.

2) *A Chronology of the U.S. Navy 1795-1965*, by David M. Cooney, USN, 1965, Franklin Watts, Inc.

3) *Empires of the Sea*, by Roger Crowley, 2008, Random House Inc.

4) *Princes of Malta*, by Charles Mula, 2000, Publishers Enterprises Group Ltd.

5) *They Must Be Stopped*, by Brigitte Gabriel, 2008, St. Martin's Press.

6) *The Blood of Lambs*, by Kamal Saleem, 2009, Howard Books.

7) *1453*, by Roger Crowley, 2005, Hyperion Books, New York.

8) *Muslim Mafia*, by David Gaubatz, 2009, WND Books.

9) *Reliance of the Traveller*, by Ahmad Ibn Lulu Ibn Al-Naqib and Noah Ha Mim Keller, 1991, Amana Publications.

10) *The Koranic Concept of War*, by General S.K. Malik, 1979, Pakistan.

# APPENDIX ONE
## CHRONOLOGICAL LIST OF THE SURAS OF THE KORAN

| Chronological Order | Traditional Order | Location of Revelation | Surah Name | Number of Verses | NOTES FROM THE QUR'AN Period Stated | Date Noted |
|---|---|---|---|---|---|---|
| 1 | 96 | Mecca | Alaq | 19 | early Makkan | S 68 designates 96 as 1st Surah * the 1st * S 68 the second |
| 2 | 68 | Mecca | Qalam | 52 | early Makkan | |
| 3 | 73 | Mecca | Muzammil | 20 | early Makkan | 11 to 10 years prior to Hijah |
| 4 | 74 | Mecca | Mudathir | 56 | early Makkan | 11 to 10 years prior to Hijah |
| 5 | 1 | Mecca | Fatehah | 7 | | |
| 6 | 111 | Mecca | Masad | 5 | early Makkan | |
| 7 | 81 | Mecca | Takwir | 29 | early Makkan | 6th or 7th in Chronology |
| 8 | 87 | Mecca | A'la | 19 | early Makkan | usually placed 8th |
| 9 | 92 | Mecca | Leyl | 21 | early Makkan | within 1st 10 - close to S 89 & S 93 |
| 10 | 89 | Mecca | Fajr | 20 | early Makkan | one of earliest - among 1st 10 |
| 11 | 93 | Mecca | Dhuha | 11 | early Makkan | close to S 89 & S 93 |
| 12 | 94 | Mecca | Sharh | 8 | early Makkan | Revealed to the Holy Prophet soon after the Surah |
| 13 | 103 | Mecca | Asr | 3 | early Makkan | |
| 14 | 100 | Mecca | Aadiyat | 11 | early Makkan | |
| 15 | 108 | Mecca | Kauthar | 3 | early Makkan | |
| 16 | 102 | Mecca | Takathur | 8 | early Makkan | |
| 17 | 107 | Mecca | Ma'un | 7 | early Makkan | Half early Makkan – other half unassociated, only 1-3, rest from Medinah |
| 18 | 109 | Mecca | Kafirun | 6 | early Makkan | |
| 19 | 105 | Mecca | Fil | 5 | early Makkan | |

| Chronological Order | Traditional Order | Location of Revelation | Surah Name | Number of Verses | NOTES FROM THE QUR'AN | |
|---|---|---|---|---|---|---|
| | | | | | Period Stated | Date Noted |
| 20 | 113 | Mecca | Falaq | 5 | early Makkan | |
| 21 | 114 | Mecca | Nas | 6 | early Makkan | |
| 22 | 112 | Mecca | Ikhlas | 4 | early Makkan | |
| 23 | 53 | Mecca | Najm | 62 | early Makkan | Except 32, from Medinah |
| 24 | 80 | Mecca | Abasa | 42 | early Makkan | |
| 25 | 97 | Mecca | Qadr | 5 | late Makkan | Or early Medinah |
| 26 | 91 | Mecca | Shams | 15 | early Makkan | |
| 27 | 85 | Mecca | Bhruj | 22 | early Makkan | Cognate with S 91 |
| 28 | 95 | Mecca | T'in | 8 | early Makkan | |
| 29 | 106 | Mecca | Qureysh | 4 | early Makkan | Associated with S105 |
| 30 | 101 | Mecca | Qariah | 11 | early Makkan | |
| 31 | 75 | Mecca | Qiyamah | 40 | early Makkan | |
| 32 | 104 | Mecca | Humazah | 9 | Makkan | |
| 33 | 77 | Mecca | Mursalat | 50 | early Makkan | Except 48, from Medinah |
| 34 | 50 | Mecca | Q'af | 45 | early Makkan | Except 38, from Medinah |
| 35 | 90 | Mecca | Balad | 20 | early Makkan | |
| 36 | 86 | Mecca | Tariq | 17 | early Makkan | |
| 37 | 54 | Mecca | Qamr | 55 | early Makkan | Except 44,45,46, form Medinah |
| 38 | 38 | Mecca | Sad | 88 | middle Makkan | |
| 39 | 7 | Mecca | A'Raf | 206 | late Makkan | Except 1 163-170, from Medinah |
| 40 | 72 | Mecca | J'nn | 28 | late Makkan | 2 years prior to Hijrah |
| 41 | 36 | Mecca | Ya'sin | 83 | early Makkan | |
| 42 | 25 | Mecca | Farqan | 77 | early Makkan | |
| 43 | 35 | Mecca | Fatir | 45 | early Makkan | |
| 44 | 19 | Mecca | Maryam | 98 | | 7 years before Hijrah |
| 45 | 20 | Mecca | Ta Ha | 135 | | 7th year before Hijrah |
| 46 | 56 | Mecca | Waqiah | 96 | early Makkan | Some portions not |
| 47 | 26 | Mecca | Shuara | 227 | middle Makkan | |
| 48 | 27 | Mecca | Naml | 93 | middle Makkan | |
| 49 | 28 | Mecca | Qasas | 88 | late Makkan | *just preccending the Hijrah / also * S 27 it at t |

| Chronological Order | Traditional Order | Location of Revelation | Surah Name | Number of Verses | NOTES FROM THE QUR'AN | |
|---|---|---|---|---|---|---|
| | | | | | Period Stated | Date Noted |
| 50 | 17 | Mecca | Israa | 111 | | 1 year before Hijrah |
| 51 | | Mecca | Yunus | 109 | late Makkan | 10 to 15 closely connected chronologically |
| 52 | | Mecca | Hud | 123 | late Makkan | 10 to 15 closely connected chronologically |
| 53 | | Mecca | Yousuf | 111 | late Makkan | (see 43) 10 to 154 closely connected chronologically |
| 54 | 15 | Mecca | Hijr | 99 | late Makkan | 10 to 15 closely connected chronologically |
| 55 | 6 | Mecca | Ana'm | 165 | late Makkan | |
| 56 | 37 | Mecca | Saffat | 182 | middle Makkan | |
| 57 | 31 | Mecca | Luqman | 34 | late Makkan | 29 to 32 related |
| 58 | 34 | Mecca | Saba | 54 | early Makkan | |
| 59 | 39 | Mecca | Zamar | 75 | late Makkan | |
| 60 | 40 | Mecca | Ghafer | 85 | late Makkan | 40 to 46 Chronologically connected |
| 61 | 41 | Mecca | Fazilat | 54 | late Makkan | 40 to 46 Chronologically connected |
| 62 | 42 | Mecca | Shura | 53 | late Makkan | 40 to 46 Chronologically connected |
| 63 | 43 | Mecca | Zukhruf | 89 | late Makkan | 40 to 46 Chronologically connected |
| 64 | 44 | Mecca | Dukhan | 59 | late Makkan | 40 to 46 Chronologically connected |
| 65 | 45 | Mecca | Jathiyah | 37 | late Makkan | 40 to 46 Chronologically connected |
| 66 | 46 | Mecca | Ahqaf | 35 | late Makkan | 40 to 46 Chronologically connected |
| 67 | 51 | Mecca | Dhariyat | 60 | early Makkan | |
| 68 | 88 | Mecca | Ghashiya | 26 | early Makkan | See 98* close in date to S 53 |
| 69 | 18 | Mecca | Kahf | 110 | Makkan | |
| 70 | 16 | Mecca | Nahl | 128 | late Makkan | |
| 71 | 71 | Mecca | Noah | 28 | early Makkan | |

| Chronological Order | Traditional Order | Location of Revelation | Surah Name | Number of Verses | NOTES FROM THE QUR'AN | |
|---|---|---|---|---|---|---|
| | | | | | Period Stated | Date Noted |
| 72 | 14 | Mecca | Ibhrahim | 52 | late Makkan | 10 to 15 closely connected chronologically |
| 73 | 21 | Mecca | Anbiya | 112 | middle Makkan | |
| 74 | 23 | Mecca | Muminun | 118 | late Makkan | |
| 75 | 32 | Mecca | Sajdah | 30 | middle Makkan | |
| 76 | 52 | Mecca | Tur | 49 | early Makkan | |
| 77 | 67 | Mecca | Mulk | 30 | middle Makkan | Just before S 69 & S 70 |
| 78 | 69 | Mecca | Haqqah | 52 | early Makkan | |
| 79 | 70 | Mecca | Maarij | 44 | e to m Makkan | |
| 80 | 78 | Mecca | Naba | 40 | early Makkan | Not so clearly as S 77 but not so late as S 76 |
| 81 | 79 | Mecca | Naziat | 46 | early Makkan | |
| 82 | 82 | Mecca | Infitar | 19 | early Makkan | |
| 83 | 84 | Mecca | Inshiqaq | 25 | early Makkan | |
| 84 | 30 | Mecca | Rum | 60 | | 7th or 6th year before the Hijrah (615/16) |
| 85 | 29 | Mecca | Ankabut | 69 | middle Makkan | |
| 86 | 83 | Mecca | Motafefin | 36 | early Makkan | |
| 87 | 2 | Medina | Baqarah | 286 | early Makkan | |
| 88 | 8 | Medina | Anfal | 75 | | Second year of Hijrah shortly after battle of Badr |
| 89 | 3 | Medina | Imran | 200 | early Madinah | AH 3 |
| 90 | 33 | Medina | Ahzab | 73 | Madinah | AH 5 & AH7 events noted |
| 91 | 60 | Medina | Mumtahana | 13 | Madinah | AH 8 |
| 92 | 4 | Medina | Nisa | 176 | early Madinah | |
| 93 | 99 | Medina | Zilzaleh | 8 | early Madinah | Or possibly late Makkan |
| 94 | 57 | Medina | Hadid | 29 | Madinah | After AH 8 |
| 95 | 47 | Medina | Muhammad | 38 | Madinah | 1st year of Hijrah * 47 to 49 on formation of Umm |
| 96 | 13 | Medina | Ra'd | 43 | late Makkan | 10 to 15 closely connected chronologically |

| Chronological Order | Traditional Order | Location of Revelation | Surah Name | Number of Verses | NOTES FROM THE QUR'AN | |
|---|---|---|---|---|---|---|
| | | | | | Period Stated | Date Noted |
| 97 | 55 | Medina | Rahman | 78 | early Makkan | Portions from Medinan |
| 98 | 76 | Medina | Ensan | 31 | early Makkan | See 68* some verses later |
| 99 | 65 | Medina | Talaq | 12 | Madinah | AH 6 |
| 100 | 98 | Medina | Beyinnah | 8 | early Madinah | Or possibly late Makkan |
| 101 | 59 | Medina | Hashr | 24 | Madinah | AH 4 |
| 102 | 24 | Medina | Nur | 64 | Madinah | AH 5-6 |
| 103 | 22 | Medina | Hajj | 78 | early Madinah | Parts revealed in early Madinah, parts in late Makkan |
| 104 | 63 | Medina | Munafiqun | 11 | Madinah | AH 5 |
| 105 | 58 | Medina | Mujadila | 22 | Madinah | Close in date to S 33* AH 5 to AH 7 |
| 106 | 49 | Medina | Hujurat | 18 | Madinah | AH 9 |
| 107 | 66 | Medina | Tahrim | 12 | Madinah | AH 7 |
| 108 | 64 | Medina | Taghabun | 18 | early Madinah | 1st year of Hijrah * maybe late Mekkan |
| 109 | 61 | Medina | Saff | 14 | Madinah | AH 3 |
| 110 | 62 | Medina | Jumah | 11 | early Madinah | AH 2 or 3 |
| 111 | 48 | Medina | Fath | 29 | Madinah | AH 6* 628 AD |
| 112 | 5 | Medina | Maidah | 120 | | Verse 3 considered by many to be the last AH 10 |
| 113 | 9 | Medina | Taubah | 129 | | 7 years after Surah 8 |
| 114 | 110 | Medina | Nasr | 3 | late Madinah | AH 11 |

# APPENDIX TWO
# PARTIAL LIST OF MOSQUES BUILT
# OVER CHRISTIAN AND OTHER TEMPLES

William Federer, author of *What Every American Needs to Know About the Qu'ran*, shares many examples from Islam's history of subjugation.

- In 630, Muhammad led 10,000 Muslim soldiers into Mecca and turned the pagans' most prominent spot, the Ka'aba, into the Masjid al-Haram Mosque.

- In 634, Rightly Guided Caliph Umar conquered Syria and turned the Christians' most prominent spot, the Church of Job, famous for being visited by Saint Silva in the fourth century, into the Mosque of Job.

- In 637, Caliph Umar conquered Hebron and turned the second-most prominent spot in Judaism, the Cave of the Patriarchs, into the Ibrahimi Mosque. (This was repeated by Saladin in 1188.)

- In 638, Muslim generals Amr ibn al-As and Khalid ibn al-Walid conquered Gaza and turned the prominent fifth-century Byzantine church into the Great Mosque of Gaza.

- In 638, Caliph Umar conquered Jerusalem. In 691, Caliph Al-Malik ordered the Dome of the Rock built on the most prominent spot in Judaism, the Temple Mount, followed by Caliph Al-Walid building the Al-Aqsa Mosque there in 705.

- In 651, Muslims conquered Persia and turned Zoroastrian temples in Bukhara and Istakhr into mosques.

- In 706, after Muslims took Damascus from the Byzantine Empire, Caliph Al-Walid turned the prominent Orthodox Church of St. John the Baptist into the Umayyad Mosque.

- In 710, Gen. Muhammad bin Qasim conquered Pakistan, defiled the prominent Sun Temple in Multan, which housed the great idol "sanam," and erected a mosque.

- In 784, after the conquest of Spain, Emir Abd ar-Rahman turned the prominent Visigothic Christian Church of Saint Vincent into the Great Aljama Mosque of Cordoba.

- After the conquest of Egypt, Caliphs al-Mamun (813-833) and al-Hakim (996–1021) turned prominent Coptic Christian churches and Jewish synagogues in Cairo into mosques.

- In 831, Muslims conquered Palermo, Sicily, and Asad ibn al-Furat turned the prominent Church of Saint Mary of the Assumption into the Great Mosque of Bal'harm.

- In 1193, Muslims conquered Delhi, India, and Qutbuddin Aibak turned the Red Citadel in Dhillika, the most prominent spot of the last Hindu rulers, into the Qutub Minar Mosque.

- From 1250-1517, Mamluk Muslims controlled the Golan Heights and used the ancient Synagogue of Katzrin as a mosque.

- In 1387, Turkish Muslims conquered Thessaloniki and turned the Katholikon Monastery and the Church of Aghia Sophia, which housed the relics of Saint Gregorios Palamas, into mosques, as Symeon of Thessaloniki recorded:

    *The greatest number of the buildings of the churches fell to them, of which the first was the Holy Church of the Savior. . . . These were trampled underfoot and the infidels rejoiced in them. . . . Most of the religious buildings in the city were despoiled, while altars were demolished and sacred things profaned.*

- On May 29, 1453, Sultan Mehmet II conquered Constantinople and turned the great Byzantine church, Hagia Sophia, into the Ayasofya Mosque. The largest church in Christendom for a thousand years, the church's four acres of gold mosaics were covered with whitewash and Quran verses.

- In 1458, Sultan Mehmet II conquered Athens and turned the Greeks' most prominent spot, the Parthenon on Acropolis hill, into a mosque. When Venetian Gen. Francesco Morosini drove the Muslims out in 1687, a cannonball hit the gunpowder stored in the mosque, blowing it up.

- In the fifteenth century, Ottoman invaders turned Saint Clement's Macedonian Orthodox Monastery in Plaosnik, Balkans, into the Imater Mosque.

- From 1519-1858, Muslim Mughal rulers gained control of India and turned over 2,000 Hindu temples into mosques, including demolishing the Temple of Ram Janmabhoomi in Ayodhya, the birthplace of Rama, and replacing it with the Babri Mosque.

India's Mughal Muslim ruler, Jahangir (1605-1627), wrote in his Tujuk-i-Jahangiri:

*At the city of Banaras [was] a temple . . . I made it my plea for throwing down the temple . . . and on the spot, with the very same materials, I erected the great mosque.*

- In 1543, Hayreddin Barbarossa's 30,000 Muslim troops wintered in Toulon, France, and turned the prominent Toulon Cathedral into a mosque.

- In 1570, under Sultan Selim II Khan, Muslims conquered Paphos, Cyprus, and Gov. Mehmet Bey Ebubkir turned the prominent Christian church into the Great Mosque of Paphos.

- In 1571, Muslims invaded Famagusta, Cyprus, and turned Saint Nicholas Cathedral, a rare Gothic church, into the Lala Mustafa Pasha Mosque, and Saint Sophia Cathedral in Nicosia, constructed in 1228, into the Selimiye Mosque.

- In 1588, Sultan Murat III turned the Eastern Orthodox Church of Saint John the Forerunner in Constantinople into the Hirami Ahmet Pasha Mosque.

- In 1781, after having conquered the Old City of Acre, Ottoman Muslims turned the Roman Catholic church built by Crusaders into the Jezzar Ahmet Pasha Mosque, where a hair from Muhammad's beard is preserved.

- In 1923, Muslims expelled Greeks from Turkey and turned Orthodox churches into mosques.

- In World War II, Nazis allied with Bosnians and turned the prominent Artists' Gallery Museum in Zagreb, Croatia into a mosque.

- In the 1950s, Muslims expelled Jews from Arab lands and turned synagogues into mosques.

- Algerian Muslims warred against French colonial rule until France pulled out in 1962, after which the Cathedral of St. Philippe was turned into the Ketchaoua Mosque. Violence against Jews caused 30,000 to flee and the Great Synagogue of Oran was turned into the Mosque Abdellah Ben Salem.

- In 1974, Turkish Muslims invaded northern Cyprus, and prominent Greek Orthodox churches were turned into mosques.

- In 1981, Muslim immigrants to the Netherlands converted Amsterdam's historic Catholic Sint-Ignatiuskerk into the Fatih Mosque, and a synagogue in The Hague into the Aksa Mosque.

- On September 11, 2001, Muslim terrorists attacked the most prominent spot in America, the World Trade Center. In less than ten years, the number of mosques in New York City has skyrocketed to more than 144.

In light of history, reasonable citizens have a right to question if the mosque proposed at Ground Zero is a sign of America's tolerance or a sign of Muslim conquest?

# APPENDIX THREE
# "AN EXPLANATORY MEMORANDUM"
written by Mohamed Akram of the Muslim Brotherhood, May 22, 1991

In the name of God, the Beneficent, the Merciful

Thanks be to God, Lord of the Two Worlds,

Prayers and peace be upon the master of the Messengers

### An Explanatory Memorandum
### On the General Strategic Goal for the Group
### In North America
### 5/22/1991

Contents:

1) An introduction in explanation

2) The Concept of Settlement

3) The Process of Settlement

4) Comprehensive Settlement Organizations

In the name of God, the Beneficent, the Merciful

Thanks be to God, Lord of the Two Worlds

And Blessed are the Pious

5/22/1991

The beloved brother/The General Masul, may God keep him

The beloved brother/Secretary of the Shura Council, may God keep him

The beloved brothers Members ofthe Shura Council, may God keep them

God's peace, mercy and blessings be upon you.... To proceed,

I ask Almighty God that you, your families and those whom you love around you are in the best of conditions, pleasing to God, glorified His name be.

I send this letter of mine to you hoping that it would seize your attention and receive your good care as you are the people of responsibility and those to whom trust is given. Between your hands is an "Explanatory Memorandum" which I put effort in writing down so that it is not locked in the chest and the mind, and so that I can share with you a portion of the responsibility in leading the Group in this country.

What might have encouraged me to submit the memorandum in this time in particular is my feeling of a "glimpse of hope" and the beginning of good tidings which bring the good news that we have embarked on a new stage of Islamic activism stages in this continent.

The papers which are between your hands are not abundant extravagance, imaginations or hallucinations which passed in the mind of one of your brothers, but they are rather hopes, ambitions and challenges that I hope that you share some or most of which with me. I do not claim their infallibility or absolute correctness, but they are an attempt which requires study, outlook, detailing and rooting from you.

My request to my brothers is to read the memorandum and to write what they wanted of comments and corrections, keeping in mind that what is between your hands is not strange or a new submission without a root, but rather an attempt to interpret and explain some of what came in the long-term plan which we approved and adopted in our council and our conference in the year (1987).

So, my honorable brother, do not rush to throw these papers away due to your many occupations and worries. All that I'm asking of you is to read them and to comment on them hoping that we might continue together the project of our plan and our Islamic work in this part of the world.

Should you do that, I would be thankful and grateful to you.

I also ask my honorable brother, the Secretary of the Council, to add the subject of the memorandum on the Council agenda in its coming meeting.

May God reward you good and keep you for His Daw'a Your brother Mohamed Akram

In the name of God, the Beneficent, the Merciful

Thanks be to God, Lord of the Two Worlds

And Blessed are the Pious

Subject: A project for an explanatory memorandum for the General Strategic goal for the Group in North America mentioned in the long-term plan.

## ONE: THE MEMORANDUM IS DERIVED FROM:

1) The general strategic goal of the Group in America which was approved by the Shura Council and the Organizational Conference for the year [1987] is "Enablement of Islam in North America, meaning: establishing an effective and a stable Islamic Movement led by the Muslim Brotherhood which adopts Muslims' causes domestically and globally, and which works to expand the observant Muslim base, aims at unifying and directing Muslims' efforts, presents Islam as a civilization alternative and supports the global Islamic State wherever it is."

2) The priority that is approved by the Shura Council for the work of the Group in its current and former session which is "Settlement."

3) The positive development with the brothers in the Islamic Circle in an attempt to reach a unity of merger.

4) The constant need for thinking and future planning, an attempt to read it and working to "shape" the present to comply and suit the needs and challenges of the future.

5) The paper of his eminence, the General Masul, may God keep him, which he recently sent to the members of the Council.

## Two: An Introduction to the Explanatory Memorandum:

In order to begin with the explanation, we must "summon" the following question and place it in front of our eyes as its relationship is important and necessary with the strategic goal and the explanation project we are embarking on. The question we are facing is: "How do you like to see the Islam Movement in North America in ten years?" or "taking along" the following sentence when planning and working, "Islamic Work in North America in the year (2000): A Strategic Vision."

Also, we must summon and take along "elements" of the general strategic goal of the Group in North America and I will intentionally repeat them in numbers. They are:

1) Establishing an effective and stable Islamic Movement led by the Muslim Brotherhood.

2) Adopting Muslims' causes domestically and globally.

3) Expanding the observant Muslim base.

4) Unifying and directing Muslims' efforts.

5) Presenting Islam as a civilization alternative.

6) Supporting the establishment of the global Islamic State wherever it is.

It must be stressed that it has become clear and emphatically known that all is in agreement that we must "settle" or "enable" Islam and its Movement in this part of the world.

Therefore, a joint understanding of the meaning of settlement or enablement must be adopted, through which and on whose basis we explain the general strategic goal with its six elements for the Group in North America.

## THREE: THE CONCEPT OF SETTLEMENT:

This term was mentioned in the Group's "dictionary" and documents with various meanings in spite of the fact that everyone meant one thing with it. We believe that the understanding of the essence is the same and we will attempt here to give the word and its "meanings" a practical explanation with a practical Movement tone, and not a philosophical linguistic explanation, while stressing that this explanation of ours is not complete until our explanation of "the process" of settlement itself is understood which is mentioned in the following paragraph. We briefly say the following:

Settlement: "That Islam and its Movement become a part of the homeland it lives in."

Establishment: "That Islam turns into firmly-rooted structure and testimony are built."

Stability: "That Islam is stable in the land on which its people move."

Enablement: "That Islam is enabled within the souls, minds and the lives of the people of the country in which it moves."

Rooting: "That Islam is resident and not a passing thing, or rooted, "entrenched," in the soil of the spot where it moves and not a strange plant to it."

## FOUR: THE PROCESS OF SETTLEMENT:

In order for Islam and its Movement to become "a part of the homeland" in which it lives, "stable" in its land, "rooted" in the spirits and minds of its people, "enabled" in the lives of its society, and has firmly-established "organizations" on which the Islamic structure is built and with which the testimony of civilization is achieved, the Movement must plan and struggle to obtain "the keys" and the tools of this process and carry out this grand mission as a "Civilization Jihadist" responsibility which lies on the shoulders of Muslims and on top of them the Muslim Brotherhood in this country. Among these keys and tools are the following:

1) **Adopting the concept of settlement and understanding its practical meanings:**

The Explanatory Memorandum focused on the Movement and the realistic dimension of the process of settlement and its practical meanings without paying attention to the difference in understanding between the resident and the non-resident, or who is the settled and the non-settled, and we believe that what was mentioned in the long-term plan in that regard suffices.

2) **Making a fundamental shift in our thinking and mentality in order to suit the challenges of the settlement mission.**

What is meant with the shift which is a positive expression is responding to the grand challenges of the settlement issues. We believe that any transforming response begins with the method of thinking and its center, the brain, first. In order to clarify what is meant with the shift as a key to qualify us to enter the field of settlement, we say very briefly that the following must be accomplished:

- A shift from the partial thinking mentality to the comprehensive thinking mentality.

- A shift from the "amputated" partial thinking mentality to the "continuous" comprehensive mentality.

- A shift from the mentality of caution and reservation to the mentality of risk and controlled liberation.

- A shift from the mentality of the elite Movement to the mentality of the popular Movement.

- A shift from the mentality of preaching and guidance to the mentality of building and testimony.

- A shift from the single opinion mentality to the multiple opinion mentality.

- A shift from the collision mentality to the absorption mentality.

- A shift from the individual mentality to the team mentality.

- A shift from the anticipation mentality to the initiative mentality.

- A shift from the hesitation mentality to the decisiveness mentality.

- A shift from the principles mentality to the programs mentality.

- A shift from the abstract ideas mentality the true organizations mentality [this is the core point and the essence of the memorandum].

**3) Understanding the historical stages in which the Islamic Ikhwani activism went through in this country:**

The writer of the memorandum believes that understanding and comprehending the historical stages of the Islamic activism which was led and being led by the Muslim Brotherhood in this continent is a very important key in working towards settlement, through which the Group observes its march, the direction of its movement and the curves and turns of its road. We will suffice here with mentioning the title for each of these stages [The title expresses the prevalent characteristic of the stage] [Details maybe mentioned in another future study]. Most likely, the stages are:

A) The stage of searching for self and determining the identity.

B) The stage of inner build-up and tightening the organization.

C) The stage of mosques and the Islamic centers.

D) The stage of building the Islamic organizations—the first phase.

E) The stage of building the Islamic schools—the first phase.

F) The stage of thinking about the overt Islamic Movement—the first phase.

G) The stage of openness to the other Islamic movements and attempting to reach a formula for dealing with them—the first phase.

H) The stage of reviving and establishing the Islamic organizations—the second phase.

We believe that the Group is embarking on this stage in its second phase as it has to open the door and enter as it did the first time.

## 4) Understanding the role of the Muslim Brother in North America:

The process of settlement is a "Civilization-Jihadist Process" with all the word means. The Ikhwan must understand that their work in America is a kind of grand Jihad in eliminating and destroying the Western civilization from within and "sabotaging" its miserable house by their hands and the hands of the believers so that it is eliminated and God's religion is made victorious over all other religions. Without this level of understanding, we are not up to this challenge and have not prepared ourselves for Jihad yet. It is a Muslim's destiny to perform Jihad and work wherever he is and wherever he lands until the final hour comes, and there is no escape from that destiny except for those who chose to slack. But, would the slackers and the Mujahedeen be equal?

## 5) Understanding that we cannot perform the settlement mission by ourselves or away from people:

A mission as significant and as huge as the settlement mission needs magnificent and exhausting efforts. With their capabilities, human, financial, and scientific resources, the Ikhwan will not be able to carry out this mission alone or away from people and he who believes that is wrong, and God knows best. As for the role of the Ikhwan, it is the initiative, pioneering, leadership, raising the banner and pushing people in that direction. They are then to work to employ, direct and unify Muslims' efforts and powers for this process. In order to do that, we must possess a mastery of the art of "coalitions," the art of "absorption" and the principles of "cooperation."

6) **The necessity of achieving a union and balanced gradual merger between private work and public work:**

We believe that what was written about this subject is many and is enough. But, it needs a time and a practical frame so that what is needed is achieved in a gradual and a balanced way that is compatible with the process of settlement.

7) **The conviction that the success of the settlement of Islam and its Movement in this country is a success to the global Islamic Movement and a true support for the sought-after state, God willing:**

There is a conviction—with which this memorandum disagrees—that our focus in attempting to settle Islam in this country will lead to negligence in our duty towards the global Islamic Movement in supporting its project to establish the state. We believe that the reply is in two segments: One: The success of the Movement in America in establishing an observant Islamic base with power and effectiveness will be the best support and aid to the global Movement project.

And the second is the global Movement has not succeeded yet in "distributing roles" to its branches, stating what is the needed from them as one of the participants or contributors to the project to establish the global Islamic state. The day this happens, the children of the American Ikhwani branch will have far-reaching impact and positions that make the ancestors proud.

8) **Absorbing Muslims and winning them with all of their factions and colors in America and Canada for the settlement project, and making it their cause, future and the basis of their Islamic life in this part of the world:**

This issue requires from us to learn "the art of dealing with the others," as people are different and people in many colors. We need to adopt the principle which says, "Take from people . . . the best they have," their best specializations, experiences, arts, energies and abilities. By people here we mean those within or without the ranks of individuals and organizations. The policy of "taking" should be with what achieves the strategic goal and the settlement process. But the big challenge in front of us is: how to connect them all in "the orbit" of our plan and "the circle" of our Movement in order to achieve "the core" of our interest. To me, there is no choice for us other than alliance and mutual understanding of those who desire from our religion and those who agree from our belief in work. And the U.S. Islamic arena is full of those waiting . . . the pioneers.

What matters is bringing people to the level of comprehension of the challenge that is facing us as Muslims in this country, conviction of our settlement project, and understanding the benefit of agreement, cooperation, and alliance. At that time, if we ask for money, a lot of it would come, and if we ask for men, they would come in lines. What matters is that our plan is "the criterion and the balance" in our relationship with others.

Here, two points must be noted; the first one: We need to comprehend and understand the balance of the Islamic powers in the U.S. arena [and this might be the subject of a future study]. The second point: what we reached with the brothers in "ICNA" is considered a step in the right direction, the beginning of good and the first drop that requires growing and guidance.

9) **Reexamining our organizational and administrative bodies, the type of leadership and the method of selecting it with what suits the challenges of the settlement mission:**

The memorandum will be silent about details regarding this item even though it is logical and there is a lot to be said about it.

10) **Growing and developing our resources and capabilities, our financial and human resources with what suits the magnitude of the grand mission:**

If we examined the human and the financial resources the Ikhwan alone own in this country, we and others would feel proud and glorious. And if we add to them the resources of our friends and allies, those who circle in our orbit and those waiting on our banner, we would realize that we are able to open the door to settlement and walk through it seeking to make Almighty God's word the highest.

**11) Utilizing the scientific method in planning, thinking and preparation of studies needed for the process of settlement:**

Yes, we need this method, and we need many studies which aid in this civilization Jihadist operation. We will mention some of them briefly:

- The history of the Islamic presence in America.

- The history of the Islamic Ikhwani presence in America.

- Islamic movements, organizations and organizations: analysis and criticism.

- The phenomenon of the Islamic centers and schools: challenges, needs and statistics.

- Islamic minorities.

- Muslim and Arab communities.

- The U.S. society: make-up and politics.

- The U.S. society's view of Islam and Muslims . . . And many other studies which we can direct our brothers and allies to prepare, either through their academic studies or through their educational centers or organizational tasking. What is important is that we start.

**12) Agreeing on a flexible, balanced and a clear "mechanism" to implement the process of settlement within a specific, gradual and balanced "time frame" that is in-line with the demands and challenges of the process of settlement.**

**13) Understanding the U.S. society from its different aspects, an understanding that "qualifies" us to perform the mission of settling our Dawa' in its country "and growing it" on its land.**

14) **Adopting a written "jurisprudence" that includes legal and movement bases, principles, policies and interpretations which are suitable for the needs and challenges of the process of settlement.**

15) **Agreeing on "criteria" and balances to be a sort of "antennas" or "the watch tower" in order to make sure that all of our priorities, plans, programs, bodies, leadership, monies and activities march towards the process of the settlement.**

16) **Adopting a practical, flexible formula through which our central work complements our domestic work.**

[Items 12 through 16 will be detailed later].

17) **Understanding the role and the nature of work of "The Islamic Center" in every city with what achieves the goal of the process of settlement:**

The center we seek is the one which constitutes the "axis" of our Movement, the "perimeter" of the circle of our work, our "balance center," the "base" for our rise and our "Dar al-Arqam" to educate us, prepare us, and supply our battalions in addition to being the "niche" of our prayers.

This is in order for the Islamic center to turn—in action not in words—into a seed "for a small Islamic society" which is a reflection and a mirror to our central organizations. The center ought to turn into a "beehive" which produces sweet honey. Thus, the Islamic center would turn into a place for study, family, battalion, course, seminar, visit, sport, school, social club, women gathering, kindergarten for male and female youngsters, the office of the domestic political resolution, and the center for distributing our newspapers, magazines, books and our audio and visual tapes.

In brief we say: we would like for the Islamic center to become "The House of Dawa" and "the general center" in deeds first before name. As much as we own and direct these centers at the continent level, we can say we are marching successfully towards the settlement of Dawa in this country.

Meaning that the "center's" role should be the same as the "mosque's" role during the time of God's prophet, God's prayers and peace be upon him, when he marched to "settle" the Dawa in its first generation in Madina. From the mosque, he drew the Islamic life and provided to the world the most magnificent and fabulous civilization humanity knew.

This mandates that, eventually, the region, the branch and the Usra turn into "operations rooms" for planning, direction, monitoring and leadership for the Islamic center in order to be a role model to be followed.

18) **Adopting a system that is based on "selecting" workers, "role distribution" and "assigning" positions and responsibilities is based on specialization, desire and need with what achieves the process of settlement and contributes to its success.**

19) **Turning the principle of dedication for the Masuls of main positions within the Group into a rule, a basis and a policy in work. Without it, the process of settlement might be stalled [Talking about this point requires more details and discussion].**

20) **Understanding the importance of the "Organizational" shift in our Movement work, and doing Jihad in order to achieve it in the real world with what serves the process of settlement and expedites its results, God Almighty's willing:**

The reason this paragraph was delayed is to stress its utmost importance as it constitutes the heart and the core of this memorandum. It also constitutes the practical aspect and the true measure of our success or failure in our march towards settlement. The talk about the organizations and the "organizational" mentality or phenomenon does not require much details. It suffices to say that the first pioneer of this phenomenon was our prophet Muhammad, God's peace, mercy, and blessings be upon him, as he placed the foundation for the first civilized organization which is the mosque, which truly became "the comprehensive organization." And this was done by the pioneer of the contemporary Islamic Dawa,' Imam martyr Hasan al-Banna, may God have mercy on him, when he and his brothers felt the need to "re-establish" Islam and its movement anew, leading him to establish organizations with all their kinds: economic, social, media, scouting, professional and even the military ones. We must say that we are in a country which understands no language other than the language of the organizations, and one which does not respect or give weight to any group without effective, functional and strong organizations.

It is good fortune that there are brothers among us who have this "trend," mentality or inclination to build the organizations who have beat us by action and words which leads us to dare say honestly what Sadat in Egypt once said, "We want to build a country of organizations"—a word of right he meant wrong with. I say to my brothers, let us raise the banner of truth to establish right "We want to establish the Group of organizations," as without it we will not able to put our feet on the true path.

And in order for the process of settlement to be completed, we must plan and work from now to equip and prepare ourselves, our brothers, our apparatuses, our sections and our committees in order to turn into comprehensive organizations in a gradual and balanced way that is suitable with the need and the reality, What encourages us to do that—in addition to the aforementioned—is that we possess "seeds" for each organization from the organization we call for [See attachment number (1)],

All we need is to tweak them, coordinate their work, collect their elements and merge their efforts with others and then connect them with the comprehensive plan we seek.

For instance, we have a seed for a "comprehensive media and art" organization: we own a print + advanced typesetting machine + audio and visual center + art production office + magazines in Arabic and English [The Horizons, The Hope, The Politicians, Ila Falastine, Press Clips, al-Zaytouna, Palestine Monitor, Social Sciences Magazines.] + art band + photographers + producers + programs anchors + journalists + in addition to other media and art experiences."

Another example:

We have a seed for a "comprehensive Dawa educational" organization: We have the Dawa section in ISNA + Dr. Jamal Badawi Foundation + the center run by brother Hamed al-Ghazali + the Dawa center the Dawa Committee and brother Shaker al-Sayyed are seeking to establish now + in addition to other Dawa efforts here and there...."

And this applies to all the organizations we call on establishing.

The big challenge that is ahead of us is how to turn these seeds or "scattered" elements into comprehensive, stable, "settled" organizations that are connected with our Movement and which fly in our orbit and take orders from our guidance. This does not prevent—but calls for—each central organization to have its local branches but its connection with the Islamic center in the city is a must.

What is needed is to seek to prepare the atmosphere and the means to achieve "the merger" so that the sections, the committees, the regions, the branches and the Usras are eventually the heart and the core of these organizations.

Or, for the shift and the change to occur as follows:

1) The Movement Department + The Organizational & Administrative Organization + The Secretariat Department The General Center

2) Education Department + Dawa Com. + Dawa and Educational Organization

3) Sisters Department  + The Women's Organization

4) The Financial Department + Investment + The Economic Organization Committee + The Endowment

5) Youth Department + Youths + Youth Organizations Organizations Department

6) The Social Committee + Matrimony + The Social Organization Committee + Mercy Foundation

7) The Security Committee - The Security Organization

8) The Political Depart. + Palestine Com. + The Political Organization

9) The Group's Court + The Legal Com. + The Judicial Organization

10) Domestic Work Department - Its work is to be distributed to the rest of the organizations

11) Our magazines + the print + The Media and Art Organization our art band

12) The Studies Association + The Intellectual & Cultural Organization Publication House + Dar al-Kitab

13) Scientific and Medial societies + Scientific, Educational & Professional Organization

14) The Organizational Conference + The Islamic-American Founding Conference

15) The Shura Council + Planning Com. + The Shura Council for the Islamic-American Movement

16) The Executive Office + The Executive Office of the Islamic-American Movement

17) The General Masul + Chairman of the Islamic Movement and its official Spokesman

18) The regions, branches & Usras + Field leaders of organizations & Islamic centers

## FIVE: COMPREHENSIVE SETTLEMENT ORGANIZATION:

We would then seek and struggle in order to make each one of these above-mentioned organizations a "comprehensive organization" throughout the days and the years, and as long as we are destined to be in this country. What is important is that we put the foundation and we will be followed by peoples and generations that would finish the march and the road but with a clearly-defined guidance.

And, in order for us to clarify what we mean with the comprehensive, specialized organization, we mention here the characteristics and traits of each organization of the "promising" organizations.

1) **From the Dawa and educational aspect [The Dawa and Educational Organization]: to include:**
   - The Organization to spread the Dawa (Central and local branches).
   - An institute to graduate Callers and Educators.
   - Scholars, Callers, Educators, Preachers and Program Anchors.
   - Art and communication technology, Conveyance and Dawa.'
   - A television station.
   - A specialized Dawa magazine.
   - A radio station.
   - The Higher Islamic Council for Callers and Educators.
   - The Higher Council for Mosques and Islamic Centers.
   - Friendship Societies with the other religions . . . and things like that.

2) **Politically [The Political Organization]: to include:**
   - A central political party.
   - Local political offices.
   - Political symbols.
   - Relationships and alliances.
   - The American Organization for Islamic Political Action
   - Advanced Information Centers . . . and things like that.

3) **Media [The Media and Art Organization]: to include:**
   - A daily newspaper.
   - Weekly, monthly and seasonal magazines.
   - Radio stations.

- Television programs.

- Audio and visual centers.

- A magazine for the Muslim child.

- A magazine for the Muslim woman.

- A print and typesetting machines.

- A production office.

- A photography and recording studio.

- Art bands for acting, chanting and theater.

- A marketing and art production office . . . and things like that.

4) **Economically [The Economic Organization]: to include:**

- An Islamic Central bank.

- Islamic endowments.

- Investment projects.

- An organization for interest free loans . . . and things like that.

5) **Scientifically and Professionally [The Scientific, Educational and Professional Organization]: to include:**

- Scientific research centers.

- Technical organizations and vocational training.

- An Islamic university.

- Islamic schools.

- A council for education and scientific research.

- Centers to train teachers.

- Scientific societies in schools.

- An office for academic guidance.

- A body for authorship and Islamic curricula . . . and things like that.

6) **Culturally and Intellectually [The Cultural and Intellectual Organization]: to include:**
   - A center for studies and research.
   - Cultural and intellectual foundations such as [The Social Scientists Society - Scientists and Engineers Society].
   - An organization for Islamic thought and culture.
   - A publication, translation and distribution house for Islamic books.
   - An office for archiving, history and authentication.
   - The project to translate the Noble Quran, the Noble Sayings . . . and things like that.

7) **Socially [The Social-Charitable Organization]: to include:**
   - Social clubs for the youths and the community's sons and daughters.
   - Local societies for social welfare and the services are tied to the Islamic centers.
   - The Islamic Organization to Combat the Social Ills of the U.S. Society.
   - Islamic houses project.
   - Matrimony and family cases office . . . and things like that.

8) **Youths [The Youth Organization]: to include:**
   - Central and local youths foundations.
   - Sports teams and clubs.
   - Scouting teams . . . and things like that.

9) **Women [The Women Organization]: to include:**
   - Central and local women societies.
   - Organizations of training, vocational and housekeeping.
   - An organization to train female preachers.
   - Islamic kindergartens . . . and things like that.

10) **Organizationally and Administratively [The Administrative and Organizational Organization]: to include:**
   - An institute for training, growth, development and planning
   - Prominent experts in this field
   - Work systems, bylaws and charters fit for running the most complicated bodies and organizations
   - A periodic magazine in Islamic development and administration.
   - Owning camps and halls for the various activities.
   - A data, polling and census bank.
   - An advanced communication network.
   - An advanced archive for our heritage and production . . . and things like that.

11) **Security [The Security Organization]: to include:**
   - Clubs for training and learning self-defense techniques.
   - A center which is concerned with the security issues [Technical, intellectual, technological and human] . . . and things like that.

12) **Legally [The Legal Organization]: to include:**
   - A Central Jurisprudence Council.
   - A Central Islamic Court.
   - Muslim Attorneys Society.
   - The Islamic Foundation for Defense of Muslims' Rights . . . and things like that.

And success is by God.

# APPENDIX FOUR
## LIST OF ORGANIZATIONS THAT ARE FRONTS FOR THE MUSLIM BROTHERHOOD

The Muslim Brotherhood's own *Explanatory Memorandum* identifies the following groups under the heading, "A list of our organizations and the organizations of our friends."

1) ISNA = ISLAMIC SOCIETY OF NORTH AMERICA

2) MSA = MUSLIM STUDENTS ASSOCIATION

3) MCA = THE MUSLIM COMMUNITIES ASSOCIATION

4) AMSS = THE ASSOCIATION OF MUSLIM SOCIAL SCIENTIST

5) AMSE = THE ASSOCIATION OF MUSLIM SCIENTISTS AND ENGINEERS

6) IMA = ISLAMIC MEDICAL ASSOCIATION

7) ITC = ISLAMIC TEACHING CENTER

8) NAIT = NORTH AMERICAN ISLAMIC TRUST

9) FID = FOUNDATION FOR INTERNATIONAL DEVELOPMENT

10) IHC = ISLAMIC HOUSING COOPERATIVE

11) ICD = ISLAMIC CENTERS DIVISION

12) ATP = AMERICAN TRUST PUBLICATIONS

13) AVC = AUDIO-VISUAL CENTER

14) IBS = ISLAMIC BOOK SERVICE

15) MBA = MUSLIM BUSINESSMEN ASSOCIATION

16) MYNA = MUSLIM YOUTH OF NORTH AMERICA

17) IFC = ISNA FIQH COMMITTEE

18) IPAC = ISNA POLITICAL AWARENESS COMMITTEE

19) IED = ISLAMIC EDUCATION DEPARTMENT

20) MAYA = MUSLIM ARAB YOUTH ASSOCIATION

21) MISG = MALASIAN [sic] ISLAMIC STUDY GROUP

22) IAP = ISLAMIC ASSOCIATION FOR PALESTINE

23) UASR = UNITED ASSOCIATION FOR STUDIES AND RESEARCH

24) OLF = OCCUPIED LAND FUND

25) MIA = MERCY INTERNATIONAL ASSOCIATION

26) ISNA = ISLAMIC CIRCLE OF NORTH AMERICA

27) BMI = BAITUL MAL INC

28) IIIT = INTERNATIONAL INSTITUTE FOR ISLAMIC THOUGHT

29) IIC = ISLAMIC INFORMATION CENTER

# APPENDIX FIVE

## ATTACHMENT A FROM THE HOLY LAND FOUNDATION TRIAL, NOV. 2008, LIST OF UNINDICTED CO-CONSPIRATORS

IN THE UNITED STATES DISTRICT COURT FOR THE NORTHERN DISTRICT OF TEXAS DALLAS DIVISION

UNITED STATES OF AMERICA VS. CR NO.

HOLY LAND FOUNDATION FOR RELIEF AND DEVELOPMENT, also known as the "HLF" (01)

SHUKRI ABU BAKER, (02)

ECF MOHAMMED EL-MEZAIN, (03)

GHASSAN ELASHI, (04)

HAITHAM MAGHAWRI, (05)

AKRAM MISHAL, (06)

MUFID ABDULQADER, (07) and

ABDULRAHMAN ODEH (08)

List of Unindicted Co-conspirators and/or Joint Venturers*

(It should be noted that certain individuals and/or entities appear in more than one category.)

I. The following are individuals/entities who are or were part of the HAMAS' social infrastructure in Israel and the Palestinian territories:

1. Abdel Al Jeneidi
2. Abdel Khalek Al Natsheh
3. Abdel Rahim Hanbali
4. Abdul Rahman Baroud
5. Adali Yaish
6. Ahmad Abdullah
7. Ahmed Al Kurd
8. Ahmed Baher
9. Akram Kharoubi
10. Alaa Anwar Aqel

125

11. Al Anwar Al Ibrahimi Library
12. Al Salah Society
13. Al Razi Hospital
14. Amal Alafranji
15. Amin Shweiki
16. Anees Shaheen
17. Aqel Rabi
18. Asaad Abu Sharkh
19. Bethlehem Orphans Society
20. Bilal Yousif Asfira
21. Ekram Taweel
22. Fallah Herzallah
23. Fatimeh Odeh
24. Fawaz Hamad, aka Abul Abed
25. Foud Abu Zeid
26. Ghassan Harmas
27. Hafeth Natsheh
28. Halhul Zakat
29. Hamad Hassanat
30. HAMAS
31. Hamed Al Bitawi
32. Hanadi Natsheh
33. Hashem Sadeq El Natsheh
34. Hatem Qafisha
35. Hoda Abdeen
36. Hosni Khawaji
37. Husni Abu Awad
38. Hussein Abu Kweik
39. Hussein Al Khatib
40. Ibrahim Abdel Rahim Dawoud, aka Bilal Hanoun
41. Ibrahim Mosleh
42. Ibrahim Al Yazuri
43. Islamic University of Gaza
44. Islamic Center of Gaza, aka Islamic Complex, aka Al Mojamma Al Islami
45. Islamic Relief Committee
46. Islamic Society of Gaza
47. Islamic Charitable Society of Hebron
48. Islamic Science and Culture Committee
49. Islamic Heritage Committee
50. Jamal Al Khodary
51. Jamal Al Tawil
52. Jamil Hammami, aka Abu Hamza
53. Jenin Zakat
54. Kamal Al Tamimi, aka Abu Islam
55. Khaled Abdelqader
56. Khalid Al Masri
57. Khalil Shaheen
58. Mahmoud Yasin Ahmed El Sheikh Yasin
59. Mahmud Rumahi
60. Mahtahdi Musleh
61. Mervit Al Masri
62. Mohamed Fouad Abu Zeid
63. Mohamed Saker
64. Mohamed Eid Misk
65. Mohamed Siam, aka Abu Mahmud
66. Mufid Mukhalalati
67. Muhamad Salman Baroud
68. Muhammad Taha
69. Muhammad Muharam
70. Muslim Womens' Society
71. Nabil Mansour
72. Nablus Zakat
73. Najeh Bakarat
74. Nasser Hidmi
75. Omar Hamdan
76. Patients Friends Society
77. Qalqilya Zakat
78. Ramallah Zakat
79. Riyad Walwil
80. Salem Salamah
81. Seham Al Quatros
82. Siham Al Masri
83. Sulieman Ighbariya
84. Taher Shreitah
85. Talal Sader
86. Tawfik ATrash
87. Tolkarem Zakat
88. Walid Jarrar
89. Young Mens' Muslim Society
90. Zaid Zakarneh
91. Ziyad Mishal
92. Zuhair Elbarasse

II. The following are individuals who participated in fund-raising activities on behalf of the Holy Land Foundation for Relief and Development:

1. Abdallah Azzam
2. Abdel Jabar Hamdan
3. Abdel Aziz Jaber
4. Abdul Muni Abu Zunt
5. Ahmed Al Kofahi
6. Ahmed Nofel
7. Ahmed Al Qattan
8. Ahmed Kafaween
9. Aziz Dweik
10. Bassam Jarrar
11. Deeb Anees
12. Faisal Malawi
13. Fathi Yakan
14. Ghazi Honeina
15. Hamed Al Bitawi

16. Hammam Saeed
17. Hamza Mansour
18. Hatem Qafisha
19. Hatem Jarrar
20. Jamal Badawi
21. Jamil Hammami, aka Abu Hamza
22. Kamal Hilbawi
23. Khalil Al Quqa
24. Mahfuz Nahnah
25. Mahmud Zahar, aka Abu Khaled
26. Majdi Aqel
27. Mohamed Siam, aka Abu Mahmud
28. Mohamed Anati
29. Mohamed Shbeir
30. Mohammed Faraj Al Ghul
31. Muharram Al Arifi
32. Mustafa Mahsur
33. Omar Sobeihi
34. Omar Al Ashqar
35. Qadi Hassan
36. Raed Saleh
37. Rashed Ghanoushi
38. Yussef Al Qaradawi

III. The following are individuals/ entities who are or were members of the US Muslim Brotherhood's Palestine Committee and/or its organizations:

1. Abdel Haleem Ashqar, aka Abdel Hassan
2. Ahmed Agha
3. Akram Kharoubi
4. Al Aqsa Educational Fund
5. American Middle Eastern League, aka AMEL
6. Ayman Ismail
7. Ayman Sharawi
8. Ayman Siraj Eddin
9. Basman Elashi
10. Bayan Elashi
11. Council on American Islamic Relations, aka CAIR
12. Dalell Mohamed
13. Fawaz Mushtaha, aka Abu Mosab
14. Fayez Idlebi
15. Ghassan Dahduli
16. Hamoud Salem
17. Hassan Sabri
18. Hazim Elashi
19. IAP Information Office
20. Ibrahim Al Samneh
21. INFOCOM

22. International Computers and Communications, aka ICC
23. Islam Siam
24. Islamic Association for Palestine in North America, aka IAP
25. Islamic Association for Palestine, aka IAP
26. Ismail Elbarasse, aka Abdul Hassan, aka Abd el Hassan
27. Ismail Jaber
28. Issam El Siraj
29. Izzat Mansour
30. Jamal Said
31. Kifah Mustapha
32. Mohamed Abbas
33. Mohamed Abu Amaria
34. Mohamed El Shorbagi
35. Mohamed Akram Adlouni
36. Mohamed Al Hanooti
37. Mohamed Jaghlit
38. Mohamed Qassam Sawallha, aka Abu Obeida
39. Mohamed Salah
40. Munzer Taleb
41. Muin Shabib
42. Nader Jawad
43. Omar Ahmad, aka Omar Yehia
44. Omar El Sobani
45. Palestine Committee
46. Rashid Qurman
47. Rasmi Almallah
48. United Association for Studies and Research, aka UASR
49. Walid Abu Sharkh
50. Walid Ranu
51. Yasser Saleh Bushnaq
52. Yousef Saleh, aka Ahmed Yousef
53. Zaher Salman, aka Osama Abdullah

IV. The following are individuals/ entities who are or were members of the Palestine Section of the International Muslim Brotherhood:

1. Abdallah Azzam
2. Abdel Rahman Abu Diyeh
3. Ahmed Nofel
4. Ali Mishal
5. Hammam Saeed
6. Hani El Jasser
7. Imad Abu Diyeh
8. Islamic Action Front
9. Issa Mohamed Ahmad

10. Jawad Al Hamad
11. Kandil Shaker
12. Khairy Al Ahga, aka Abu Obeida
13. Khalid Taqi Al Din
14. Mohamed Abu Fares
15. Mohamed Eweida
16. Munir Elashi
17. Muslim Brother, aka Ikwan Al Muslimi
18. Mustafa Mahsur
19. Rageh El Kurdi
20. Ziad Abu Ghanimeh

V. The following are individuals who are and/or were leaders of HAMAS inside the Palestinian territories:

1. Abdel Aziz Rantisi
2. Ahmed Yassin
3. Ibrahim Al Yazuri
4. Imad Aqel
5. Ismail Abu Shanab
6. Ismail Haniya
7. Mahmud Al Rumahi
8. Mahmud Zahar, aka Abu Khaled
9. Muhammad Taha
10. Salah Shehadah

VI. The following are individuals who are or were leaders of the HAMAS Political Bureau and/or HAMAS leaders and/or representatives in various Middle Eastern/ African countries:

1. Ibrahim Ghoshe
2. Imad Alami
3. Khalid Mishal, aka Abu Walid
4. Mousa Abu Marzook, aka Abu Omar
5. Jamal Issa, aka Jamal Abu Baker
6. Mohamed Siyam

VII. The following are individuals/ entities who are and/or were members of the US Muslim Brotherhood:

1. Abdel Rahman Alamoudi
2. Gaddor Ibrahim Saidi
3. Islamic Society of North America, aka ISNA
4. Muslim Arab Youth Association, aka MAYA
5. Nizar Minshar

6. North American Islamic Trust, aka NAIT
7. Raed Awad
8. Tareq Suwaidan

VIII. The following are individuals/ entities that are or were part of the Global HAMAS financing mechanism:

1. Al Aqsa Society
2. Abdel Rahim Nasrallah
3. Association de Secours Palestinians
4. Commiti De Bienfaisance et de Secours aux Palestinians, aka CBSP
5. Interpal
6. Jersualem Fund, aka IRFAN
7. K & A Overseas Trading
8. Khairy Al Ahga, aka Abu Obeida
9. Palestine Relief and Development Fund
10. Palestine and Lebanon Relief Fund
11. Palestinian Association of Austria
12. Sanabil Foundation for Relief and Development
13. Soboul Al Khair

IX. The following are other individuals/entities that Marzook utilized as a financial conduit on behalf or for the benefit of HAMAS:

1. Bashir Elashi
2. Gaddor Ibrahim Saidi
3. INFOCOM
4. International Computers and Communications, aka ICC
5. K & A Overseas Trading
6. Khairy Al Ahga, aka Abu Obeida
7. Mohamed Salah
8. Munir Elashi
9. Nadia Elashi
10. Omar Salah Badahdah

X. The following are individuals who were HLF employees, directors, officers and/or representatives:

1. Abdel Jabar Hamdan
2. Ahmed Agha
3. Akram Kharoubi
4. Amal Alafranji
5. Amin Shweiki
6. Anees Shaheen
7. Asaad Abu Sharkh
8. Ayman Ismail
9. Basman Elashi

10. Dalell Mohamed
11. Ekram Taweel
12. Fatimeh Odeh
13. Fawaz Hamad, aka Abul Abed
14. Ghassan Harmas
15. Hanadi Natsheh
16. Hazim Elashi
17. Hoda Abdeen
18. Hussein Al Khatib
19. Islam Siam
20. Jamal Al Khodary
21. Kamal Al Tamimi, aka Abu Islam
22. Khalid Al Masri
23. Mervit Al Masri
24. Mohamed Dahroug
25. Mohamed Eid Misk
26. Mufid Mukhalalati
27. Muhammad Muharram
28. Kifah Mustapha
29. Mohamed Anati
30. Mohamed El Shorbagi
31. Omar Kurdi
32. Raed Awad
33. Ramzi Abu Baker
34. Rasmi Almallah
35. Seham Al Quatros
36. Sharif Battiki
37. Siham Al Masri
38. Taqi Al Din
39. Zuhair Elbarasse

XI. The following are HAMAS members whose families received support from the HLF through the HAMAS social infrastructure:

1. Adel Awadallah
2. Abdel Rahman Arouri
3. Abdel Aziz Rantisi

4. Ahmed Yassin
5. Ismail Abu Shanab
6. Ismail Haniya
7. Jamil Al Baz
8. Kamal Naeem
9. Khalil Al Quqa
10. Khamis Zaki Akel
11. Naser Ghazi Edweidar
12. Salah Eldin Nijmi
13. Salah Othman
14. Salah Shehadah
15. Yasser Hassanat
16. Yasser Namruti
17. Yehia Ayyash
19. Islam Siam
20. Jamal Al Khodary
21. Kamal Al Tamimi, aka Abu Islam
22. Khalid Al Masri
23. Mervit Al Masri
24. Mohamed Dahroug
25. Mohamed Eid Misk
26. Mufid Mukhalalati
27. Muhammad Muharram
28. Kifah Mustapha
29. Mohamed Anati
30. Mohamed El Shorbagi
31. Omar Kurdi
32. Raed Awad
33. Ramzi Abu Baker
34. Rasmi Almallah
35. Seham Al Quatros
36. Sharif Battiki
37. Siham Al Masri
38. Taqi Al Din
39. Zuhair Elbarasse

# APPENDIX SIX
# DIRECTIVE FOR THE DISESTABLISHMENT OF STATE SHINTO

Directive for the Disestablishment of State Shinto

Orders from the Supreme Commander for the Allied Powers to the Japanese Government:

15 December 1945

MEMORANDUM FOR: Imperial Japanese Government

THROUGH: Central Liaison Office, Tokyo

SUBJECT: Abolition of Governmental Sponsorship, Support, Perpetuation, Control, and Dissemination of State Shinto

1. In order to free the Japanese people from direct or indirect compulsion to believe or profess to believe in a religion or cult officially designated by the state, and in order to lift from the Japanese people the burden of compulsory financial support of an ideology which has contributed to their war guilt, defeat, suffering, privation, and present deplorable condition, and

In order to prevent recurrence of the perversion of Shinto theory and beliefs into militaristic and ultra-nationalistic propaganda designed to delude the Japanese people and lead them into wars of aggression, and

In order to assist the Japanese people in a rededication of their national life to building a new Japan based upon ideals of perpetual peace and democracy,

It is hereby directed that:

a. The sponsorship, support, perpetuation, control, and dissemination of Shinto by the Japanese national, prefectual, and local governments, or by public officials, subordinates, and employees acting in their official capacity are prohibited and will cease immediately.

b. All financial support from public funds and all official affiliation with Shinto and Shinto shrines are prohibited and will cease immediately.

c. All propagation and dissemination of militaristic and ultra-nationistic ideology in Shinto doctrines, practices, rites, ceremonies, or observances, as well as in the doctrines, practices, rites, ceremonies and observances of any other religion, faith, sect, creed, or philosophy, are prohibited and will cease immediately.

d. The Religious Functions Order relating to the Grand Shrine of Ise and the Religious Functions Order relating to State and other Shrines will be annulled.

e. The Shrine Board of the Ministry of Home Affairs will be abolished, and its present functions, duties, and administrative obligations will not be assumed by any other governmental or tax-supported agency.

f. All public educational institutions whose primary function is either the investigation and dissemination of Shinto or the training of a Shinto priesthood will be abolished and their physical properties diverted to other uses. Their present functions, duties, and administrative obligations will not be assumed by any other governmental or tax-supported agency.

g. Private educational institutions for the investigation and dissemination of Shinto and for the training of priesthood for Shinto will be permitted and will operate with the same privileges and be subject to the same controls and restrictions as any other private educational institution having no affiliation with the government; in no case, however, will they receive support from public funds, and in no case will they propagate and disseminate militaristic and ultra-nationalistic ideology.

h. The dissemination of Shinto doctrines in any form and by any means in any educational institution supported wholly or in part by public funds is prohibited and will cease immediately.

1) All teachers' manuals and text-books now in use in any educational institution supported wholly or in part by public funds will be censored, and all Shinto doctrine will be deleted. No teachers' manual or text-book which is published in the future for use in such institutions will contain any Shinto doctrine.

2) No visits to Shinto shrines and no rites, practices, or ceremonies associated with Shinto will be conducted or sponsored by any educational institution supported wholly or in part by public funds.

i. Circulation by the government of "The Fundamental Principles of the National Structure," "The Way of the Subject," and all similar official volumes, commentaries, interpretations, or instructions on Shinto is prohibited.

j. The use in official writings of the terms "Greater East Asia War," "The Whole World under One Roof," and all other terms whose connotation in Japanese is inextricably connected with State Shinto, militarism, and ultra-nationalism is prohibited and will cease immediately.

k. God-shelves (kamidana) and all other physical symbols of State Shinto in any office, school institution, organization, or structure supported wholly or in part by public funds are prohibited and will be removed immediately.

l. No official, subordinate, employee, student, citizen, or resident of Japan will be discriminated against because of his failure to profess and believe in or participate in any practice, rite, ceremony, or observance of State Shinto or of any other religion.

m. No official of the national, prefectural, or local government, acting in his public capacity, will visit any shrine to report his assumption of office, to report on conditions of government, or to participate as a representative of government in any ceremony or observance.

The purpose of this directive is to separate religion from the state to prevent misuse of religion for political ends, and to put all religions, faiths, and creeds upon exactly the same legal basis, entitled to precisely the same opportunities and protection. It forbids affiliation with the government and the propagation and dissemination of militaristic and ultra-nationalistic ideology not only to Shinto but to the followers of all religions, faiths, sects, creeds, or philosophies.

The provisions of this directive will apply with equal force to all rites, practices, ceremonies, observances, beliefs, teachings, mythology, legends, philosophy, shrines, and physical symbols associated with Shinto.

The term State Shinto within the meaning of this directive will refer to that branch of Shinto which by official acts of the Japanese Government has been differentiated from the religion of Shrine Shinto and has been classified as a non-religious national cult commonly known as State Shinto or National Shinto.

The term Shrine Shinto will refer to that branch of Shinto which by popular belief, legal commentary, and the official acts of the Japanese Government has been recognized to be a religion.

Pursuant to the terms of Article I of the Basic Directive on "Removal of Restrictions on Political, Civil, and Religious Liberties" issued on 4 October 1945 by the Supreme Commander for the Allied Powers in which the Japanese people were assured complete religious freedom,

(1) Shrine Shinto will enjoy the same protection as any other religion.

(2) Shrine Shinto, after having been divorced from the state and divested of its militaristic and ultra-nationalistic elements, will be recognized as a religion if its adherents so desire and will be granted the same protection as any other religion in so far as it may in fact be the philosophy or religion of Japanese individuals.

Militaristic and ultra-nationalistic ideology, as used in this directive, embraces those teachings, beliefs, and theories, which advocate or justify a mission on the part of Japan to extend its rule over other nations and peoples by reason of:

(1) The doctrine that the Emperor of Japan is superior to the heads of other states because of ancestry, descent, or special origin.

(2) The doctrine that the people of Japan are superior to the people of other lands because of ancestry, descent, or special origin.

(3) The doctrine that the islands of Japan are superior to other lands because of divine or special origin.

(4) Any other doctrine which tends to delude the Japanese people into embarking upon wars of aggression or to glorify the use of force as an instrument for the settlement of disputes with other people.

The Imperial Japanese Government will submit a comprehensive report to this Headquarters not later than 15 March 1946 describing in detail all action taken to comply with all provisions of this directive.

All officials, subordinates and employees of the Japanese national prefectural, and local governments, all teachers and education officials and all citizens and residents of Japan will be held personally accountable for compliance with the spirit as well as the letter of all provisions of this directive.

For the Supreme Commander:

[Signed] H. W. Allen

Colonel, A.G.D.,

Asst. Adjutant General

Website: www.nicholaspapanicolaou.com

Contact: info@nicholaspapanicolaou.com

 facebook.com/nfpapanic

 twitter.com/nfpapanic

 youtube.com/nfpapanic